THE ILLUSTRATED HISTORY OF
HELICOPTERS

Andy Lightbody ● Joe Poyer

Publications International, Ltd.

Louis Weber, C.E.O.
Publications International, Ltd.
7373 North Cicero Avenue
Lincolnwood, Illinois 60646

Permission is never granted for commercial purposes.

Printed in Yugoslavia, by Zrinski

h g f e d c b a

ISBN 0-88176-652-6

Library of Congress Catalog Card Number: 89–63617

Contributing writers

Andy Lightbody coauthored *The Illustrated History of Tanks*. He is also Editorial Director for *International Defense & Aerospace Magazine* and is the Military/Aerospace Editor for CBS Radio. Mr. Lightbody's articles appear frequently in the national and military trade press.

Joe Poyer, noted military affairs journalist and novelist, coauthored *The Illustrated History of Tanks*. He contributes regularly to numerous military publications, including *International Defense Images* and *International Combat Arms*. Mr. Poyer is currently working with Andy Lightbody on a series of books, an *Encyclopedia of Terrorism*.

Front cover: American AH-1 HueyCobra. **Back cover** (clockwise from lower left): American UH-1 Huey. American AH-64 Apache. American AH-64 Apache. American 530MG Defender. **Page 3:** American AH-1S HueyCobra. **Page 4:** American CH-47 Chinook. **Page 5** (from left to right): French Ecureuil AS 350. American UH-60A Black Hawk.

CONTENTS

Introduction: The Helicopter in War and Peace   6

CONTENTS

SOVIET UNION

GREAT BRITAIN

FRANCE

WEST GERMANY

ITALY

INTRODUCTION: THE HELICOPTER IN WAR AND PEACE

For most of Western history, vertical ascent has been a dream that first found reality in the uncontrolled flight of the hot air balloon. The helicopter came of age when the combination of technology and war provided the means as well as the need. The first practical vehicles capable of controlled vertical ascent and horizontal flight were designed and built in Nazi Germany, in preparation for a war of conquest.

Today, the helicopter has become indispensable. Anyone living in today's urban areas is familiar with the periodic traffic reports delivered by helicopter-borne radio broadcasters: "The I-5 is a mess today from Lincoln to the El Toro Y. Suggest you try alternate routes." Nearly every police department of any size and most county sheriff and state highway patrols are now equipped with helicopters for routine patrol work. Using ambient light enhancing vision aides and powerful searchlights, the police have expanded their ability to more efficiently patrol wider, more densely populated areas.

Oil companies use helicopters to ferry workers and equipment to offshore oil fields, increasing efficiency and reducing pollution. Helicopters are used by ranchers to survey fences and by power and telephone companies to check and perform maintenance on remote power lines, transmitters, and repeater stations. Helicopters are used to haul water to fight forest fires. Water district engineers use helicopters to measure snowfall in high mountains and thus predict and control water usage. Cargo-carrying helicopters have enabled Soviet engineers and settlers to open up vast stretches of Siberia. Helicopters towing magnetometers are widely used for mineral, oil, and gas exploration. The list of uses to which the helicopter has been put are virtually endless.

The helicopter has transformed war as well. Beginning with the Korean War, the helicopter has become vital to the reconnaissance, air ambulance, troop insertion, close ground support, amphibious landing, cargo and troop transport, and anti-armor roles. Rules of engagement are being written for anti-air helicopters—helicopters capable of engaging other helicopters as well as fixed wing aircraft.

History of the Helicopter's Development

The helicopter's origins can be found in China, when that nation was old but the rest of the world was young. Some 2,000 years ago, someone in China probably watched falling sycamore seeds whirling in the breeze and then built a paper model. Eventually, a gyrocopter developed from the model, and this child's toy endured for centuries. But Leonardo da Vinci (1452–1519) is credited with inventing the helicopter, as distinct from the gyrocopter. A manuscript of his known as the *Codex Atlanticus* illustrates a human-powered machine in which an "air screw" accelerates air downward. But da Vinci's helicopter, like his ornithopter, lacked a mechanical means to provide power.

The Achievement of Vertical Flight

The 1700s were a pivotal time in the development of manned vertical flight. In 1754, Mikhail Lomonosov, a Russian scientist, built a working model of an air screw. Other experiments led to the development of the hot air balloon. In 1785, two French experimenters, Launoy and Bienvenu, built a small helicopter capable of vertical flight. They stuck goose feathers into a cork fitted loosely to a stick. A leather cord wound round the stick was attached to a bow. When the bow was pulled, the stick spun and the cork and feather helicopter rose. Immediately, a major problem in powered helicopter flight was encountered—torque. The feathered cork moved sideways as fast as it rose vertically.

Torque turns the body of a helicopter in the direction opposite to the spinning blades. If this is allowed to happen, the helicopter will spin out of control. Launoy and Bienvenu solved this by using used two rotors, each turning in the opposite direction, to power their helicopter. The opposing torques canceled each other out. Opposing rotors remained the preferred method for dealing with torque for the next 150 years.

In the late 1800s, more helicopter experiments took place. By this time, relatively lightweight steam engines offered a substitute for muscle power. A Frenchman, Ponton d'Amercourt, and an Italian, Enrico Forlanini, both built steam-powered helicopter models using counterrotating blade assemblies. But the engines were too heavy to allow the helicopters to fly. In 1871, a mechanism for adjusting the cyclic pitch (angle) of helicopter blades was developed. Three years later, Achenbach described a plan for a vertical tail rotor to counteract torque.

Most of the mechanisms needed for helicopter flight—main and tail rotors, pitch control, and mechanical power—had now been invented. Only a lightweight engine was still needed—an engine that developed more power than needed to lift itself. A variety of concepts were tried, including engines powered by such exotic fuels as ether and gun cotton. In 1876, Daimler and Benz perfected the internal combustion engine. By 1903, it had been reduced in size and weight to the point where the Wright Brothers were able to achieve powered fixed wing flight. This success galvanized all areas of manned flight, including helicopter development.

Manned Vertical Flight

The first successful helicopter to achieve manned vertical flight flew in France in 1907. It was the Breguet-Richet No. 1, built in the form of a cross. A 45-horsepower gasoline engine powered four rotors on each arm of the cross. It lifted itself and a pilot three feet off the ground. But the machine was so ungainly that it had to be steadied by its ground crew. A few weeks later, Paul Corneau flew a much simpler and lighter design. Constructed in the shape of a framework V, it had two twin-blade, counterrotating blades on either end. Corneau's machine, powered by a 24-horsepower gasoline engine achieved stable flight for a few seconds.

Danish physicist J.C.H. Ellenhammer solved the problem of directional control with his manned coaxial helicopter (counterrotating blades mounted one above the other) by applying cyclic control to the rotor. In 1909, Igor I. Sikorsky, living and working in Russia and already well-known for his fixed wing aircraft designs, began a series of helicopter experiments that lasted until 1917 when he left Russia during the Revolution. None of his designs performed as he had anticipated, and in the United States he resumed his work on fixed wing aircraft.

Two other contributors to manned vertical flight were Spanish, Raoul Pescara and Don Juan de la Cierva. Between 1921 and 1926, Pescara developed a coaxial helicopter whose rotors could freewheel in case of engine trouble. This converted the helicopter to a gyrocopter and allowed it to descend under control. Pescara also developed the linkages that allow a helicopter blade to change pitch.

Don Juan de la Cierva was a well-known designer of fixed wing aircraft. After discarding the ornithopter as unworkable, Cierva turned to the gyrocopter concept. His first gyrocopter was the C-4, which he called an autogiro. It flew for the first time in January 1923. The autogiro was a fixed wing aircraft with a pusher propeller and a large four-bladed rotor mounted above the cockpit. The pusher propeller's engine supplied forward motion, and the flow of air through the rotor blades caused the blades to spin, providing lift. Later, Cierva geared the engine to provide power to the rotor as well as the pusher propeller, making vertical ascent possible. How much further Cierva might have gone in developing this dual approach to helicopter flight will never be known. He was killed in 1936 when a fixed wing passenger aircraft stalled during a takeoff from London's Croydon airport.

Top left: Paul Corneau, a French aeronautical experimenter, made the first free, untethered helicopter flight in November 1907. **Bottom right:** Don Juan de la Cierva was an early proponent of the autogiro, as opposed to the helicopter. He demonstrated his autogiro at Templehoff airfield in Berlin in 1932.

Early Military Interest in Helicopters

Throughout the 1920s, interest in helicopter development continued to grow, particularly among the military. In 1922 under a United States Army contract, George De Bothezat, who had left Russia after the Revolution, built and flew a four rotor helicopter based on Louis Breguet's design. The four rotors gave the machine a high degree of inertia, and it flew very slowly. The Army canceled the project two years later.

In 1923, the British War Office offered a £50,000 prize for a vertical flight aircraft that could fly at 60 miles per hour, achieve 2,000 feet altitude, and remain airborne for one hour. The helicopter that came closest to winning was a single rotor design built by Louis Brennan of Ireland. Brennan's design eliminated torque by mounting the engine above the fuselage on special bearings and vertically mounting propellers on the end of each horizontal blade.

So far, all helicopter designs had been multibladed. In 1924, Dutch scientist A.G. von Baumhauer built the first single main rotor helicopter. Von Baumhauer eliminated the effects of torque by mounting at the end of a long tail boom a single vertical propeller driven by a separate engine. The propeller pushed against the tail boom, and the boom acted like a lever pushing against the torque and canceling it. The concept was advanced for the time. But von Baumhauer, one of the true pioneers in helicopter design, never obtained sufficient funding to work out the many design problems that remained. However, the importance of the first operating single main rotor helicopter employing a tail rotor cannot be understated.

7

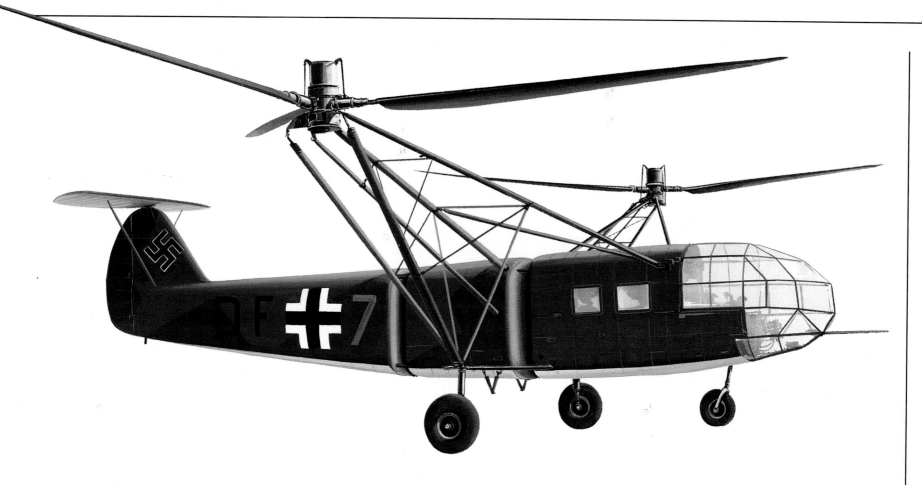

Clouds of War

In the late 1930s, helicopter design spurted ahead in two countries, Germany and the United States. The rapid progress was due primarily to two men.

The first was a citizen of Germany, where vast sums of money were spent on the development of new military hardware. Any promising weapon concept was funded. Dr. Heinrich Focke, the Focke in the famous firm of Focke-Wulf, left that company to build helicopters. Focke's first flying design used the fuselage from a small fixed wing aircraft, the Fa 61, rebuilt as a side-by-side helicopter. It made its first flight in 1937.

Dr. Focke was soon at work on an advanced version of this design. The most successful was the Focke Achgelis Fa 223. The Fa 223 was powered by a BMW-323 620 horsepower engine, weighed 9,500 pounds, and had a twin, side-by-side rotor configuration with cyclic pitch control. But the pitch control had only two settings: 13 degrees for powered flight, 8 degrees for unpowered flight, during which time the craft became a gyrocopter.

Focke's design spurred a renewed interest in helicopter flight and convinced the German military that the helicopter was a viable aircraft. Germany became the first nation to use helicopters in military service.

The German government ordered a military version, the Fa 223 Drach; it was the first helicopter designed directly for military service. But conflicting and changing priorities, coupled with technical problems, delayed production of the Fa 223. Only 20 were ever built. The German Navy contracted with Anton Flettner to build a helicopter that could be carried aboard ship for antisubmarine work. To save valuable shipping space, Flettner designed a side-by-side configuration in which the main rotor shafts were set at an eleven-degree angle from the vertical so that the blades intermeshed through special gearing, like an egg beater.

The second man to have a significant effect on helicopter design was Igor I. Sikorsky, a Russian native who continued his helicopter experiments in the United States after leaving Russia in 1917. In 1931, Sikorsky patented a single rotor helicopter; it was built in 1939 and designated the VS-300. The VS-300 is perhaps the most significant design in the history of helicopters. Sikorsky showed that a single rotor helicopter could achieve efficient flight. Sikorsky borrowed von Baumhauer's vertical revolving tail rotor to counter torque and refined the main rotor mechanism. Sikorsky himself first flew the VS-300 in 1939.

Sikorsky used a Lycoming 75-horsepower engine that drove the main rotor via five belt pulleys. By early 1941, a 100 horsepower Franklin

This page: The first helicopter placed in production was the German Focke Achgelis Fa 223 Drach, a transport helicopter.

engine had been substituted. If the craft's engine failed, the rotor could freewheel the VS-300 to a landing. Dozens of modifications were made to the VS-300 during its four-year development. The United States Army ordered an improved version of the VS-300 as its first operational helicopter, the R-4. The first production models of the R-4 were powered by a 180-horsepower engine.

American Helicopters in World War II

The R-4 was only the second helicopter to see military service during World War II and was the first to achieve air evacuation from behind enemy lines. An R-4 of the First Air Commando Group based at Hailakandi, India, flew into Burma to rescue the pilot of a light aircraft and four casualties he had been flying out in a fixed wing aircraft that crashed. The R-4 rescued the five men from a rice paddy.

In January 1945, General George E. Stratemyer, commander of American forces in the China-Burma-India Theater, requested and received six helicopters to form an air rescue squadron. The Army had been so impressed with the success of the R-4 that they had contracted with Vought-Sikorsky for a larger helicopter. Five XR-5 helicopter prototypes were built, followed by 26 YR-5s, two of which were provided to General Stratemyer before they had completed testing. The R-5 was a two-man, three-bladed helicopter that employed a tandem seating arrangement; the pilot sat behind and above the observer. The cockpit was enclosed in a clear plastic bubble. It had provision for fixing two stretchers, one on either side of the fuselage.

The helicopter was originally developed by and for the United States Army Air Force, a designation that is somewhat confusing today. During World War II, the Air Force was part of the Army, but its operations were not subordinate to Army field commanders. Near the end of the war, the

Army realized the important tactical role the helicopter could play in ground operations. Through negotiations with the Air Force, it was agreed that the Army could have its own helicopter pilots and helicopters.

Postwar Helicopter Development in the United States

United States military annual spending dropped from $80.5 billion in 1945 to $9 billion by 1950. Helicopter development was caught in this cost squeeze, and the military provided only part of the funding needed for helicopter development.

But a number of companies saw a rosy commercial future for the helicopter. Igor Sikorsky pushed ahead with the S-51, a civilian version of the R-5. In the immediate postwar years, the S-51 was pressed into lifesaving work and flew the airmail from ports in Los Angeles and London, gaining much favorable media attention.

The Bell Aircraft Company had achieved a wide measure of wartime fame with its P-39 Airacobra fighter and its P-59 Airacomet. As early as 1943, Bell had been working on a helicopter design. In December 1945, the Bell Model 47 made its maiden flight and wrote a chapter in helicopter history. The Bell 47 is perhaps the most recognizable helicopter ever built. It has a large plastic bubble canopy enclosing the three-man cockpit, an open framework tail boom with a horizontally mounted tail rotor, and a single, two-bladed main rotor.

The Model 47 was used by the military services of more than 48 nations. In civilian use, the excellent visibility afforded by its plastic nose made it popular with law enforcers, crop dusters, geological surveyors,

and forest rangers. During the Korean War, the Bell Model 47 served as the H-13 (Army) and the HTL-4 (Marine Corps). More than 6,000 Model 47s were eventually built by Bell and its various licensees.

Howard Hughes—millionaire, playboy, recordholding pilot, and industrialist—also saw a bright future for helicopters. His factory started out making drilling bits for the oil industry and then moved into fixed wing aviation. In the postwar years, the company established a helicopter division that designed and built the Hughes Models 269 and 360. Both were small utility helicopters that later found military applications.

Another company, United Helicopters Incorporated, owned by Stanley Hiller, Jr., flew its first experimental helicopter during World War II. Hiller developed a coaxial rotor helicopter designated the XH-44, and he flew it for the first time in August 1944.

Development work for the military application of helicopters continued, but at substantially reduced levels. The Piasecki Helicopter Corporation (purchased in 1956 by Boeing, becoming the Vertol Division of Boeing) flew the PV-3 "Flying Banana" in March 1945. The "Flying

Banana," so called because of the flattened "V" shape formed by its fuselage, was powered by a 600-horsepower Pratt & Whitney Wasp radial piston engine. The Navy, Marine Corps, and Coast Guard all purchased it, and it was designated the HRP-1. Piasecki favored the tandem rotor arrangement; In this design, the rotors are mounted at opposite ends of the fuselage and turn in the opposite direction to eliminate torque. The Air Force ordered a more powerful version of the PV-3, the H-21. The Army ordered 334 H-21C Shawnees. A version also went to the French Army, who used them in Algeria as armed troop transports.

The Kaman Aircraft Corporation built a twin-rotor, intermeshing blade design that made its maiden flight in 1947. The pilot could change the blade pitch in the Kaman K-125A by activating flaps on the trailing edges of each of the four blades. Kaman also designed the K-225, the first helicopter to use the Boeing YT50 gas turbine engine, in 1951. Kaman's intermeshing rotor helicopters have been a mainstay of sea rescue work for the Air Force and Navy since the early 1950s.

This page: The Bell Helicopter Model 47, shown here fitted with pontoons, is perhaps the best-known helicopter design in the world.

In 1947, the United States Marine Corps organized its first helicopter squadron and equipped it with two Sikorsky HO3S-1s, which was the naval version of the R-5. While the HO3S series proved far too small to ferry meaningful numbers of troops for amphibious landings, the squadron did demonstrate the viability of over-the-horizon assaults.

Also during this postwar period, the helicopter was investigated for its naval possibilities. The first United States helicopter to serve aboard a naval vessel under actual seagoing conditions was a Sikorsky R-4, designated HNS-1 by the Navy. This helicopter, which actually belonged to the Coast Guard, was assigned aboard the USS *Midway*. The HNS-1 was put through its paces to prove its ability to perform scouting and sea rescue work in the Arctic Ocean.

The Nazis had used the Flettner FL-282 helicopter for antisubmarine work in the latter stages of World War II, particularly in the Baltic, Adriatic, and Aegean seas. The German Navy also developed the technique of winching helicopters down on the decks of ships in heavy seas. The helicopter extended a ship's eyes and ears by 100 miles in any direction; thus, the ability to carry a helicopter aboard a ship increased the efficiency of small vessels for antisubmarine warfare (ASW).

The development of a dipping sonar device brought the helicopter to the forefront in ASW. The helicopter flies over the area where it is

suspected a submarine is located. A passive sonar probe attached to a cable is unreeled from the helicopter and dipped below the water's surface to listen for the submarine. The helicopter being airborne, the submarine detects only the intermittent and low noises of the probe penetrating the water, the ripples created by the helicopter's rotors, and the small wake created by the cable. The helicopter can also use active sonar to locate its quarry. Once the submarine has been located, the helicopter can call in surface vessels or fixed wing aircraft or launch torpedoes or mines itself.

Also during the postwar period, the Navy investigated using helicopters for plane guard duties and reconnaissance/observation. In plane guard duty, an aircraft orbits an aircraft carrier ready to drop lifesaving equipment to air crew who crash during takeoff or landing. The helicopter, with its ability to hover and lift people by winch, proved ideal for the job. Helicopters also started to replace fixed wing aircraft for observation duties.

Postwar Helicopter Development in the Soviet Union

In the years before World War II, the Soviet Army had investigated using helicopters as military weapons. After determining that helicopter design was not yet sufficiently advanced, the Soviet Army turned to the

autogiro. The Kaskr-I was designed and built by two men. N.I. Kamov was one of these two men, and his name would become virtually synonymous with helicopter design in the Soviet Union. Kamov and his research partner, N.K. Shrizhinsky, worked on several helicopter developments during the 1930s and the War. But other design and development projects carried a higher priority. The first Soviet helicopter, the Yak-100, did not fly until 1947.

The Yak-100 was virtually a copy of the Sikorsky R-5. But by the time the Yak-100 had completed testing, Mikhail Mil's design bureau had placed their Mi-1 (later codenamed Hare by NATO) into production. The Hare looked quite a bit like the British Bristol (later Westland) Sycamore. It was used by the Soviets as a light helicopter.

In 1951, Stalin ordered the two major Soviet aircraft designers, the Mil and Yakolev bureaus, to design a large transport helicopter within one year. The result was the Yakolev Yak-24 (NATO codenamed Horse) for which Mil designed and built the main rotor. The fore and aft rotors counterrotated to eliminate torque.

In 1957, one of the largest helicopters in the world went into operation. The Mi-6 (NATO codenamed Hook) weighed 60,055 pounds *empty* and was powered by two 5,500 horsepower Soloviev D-25V turboprop engines. The Mi-6, which is used by the Soviet Army as an assault, transport, and heavy-lift helicopter, can carry 68 fully equipped troops. The Mi-2 appeared in 1961 and was essentially an Mi-1 powered by two gas turbine engines. The Mi-4 Hound, also developed by the Mil design bureau, was a medium-lift helicopter. The Mi-4 resembles the Sikorsky H-19 Chickasaw but is larger and more powerful and can carry more than twice the payload.

The Soviet Navy also found uses for the helicopter. The Ka-20 (NATO codenamed Harp) from the Kamov design bureau was the first helicopter in the Soviet Union to be developed for antisubmarine and antiship warfare. The radar-equipped Ka-20 carried machine guns and air-to-surface rockets. Further development resulted in the Ka-25 (NATO codenamed Hormone), which is the mainstay of the Soviet naval helicopter fleet today. A further improvement on this basic design is the Ka-27 (NATO codenamed Helix), which carries a magnetic anomaly detection system for antisubmarine warfare.

Helicopters in the Battlefield: Korea

Between 1936 and 1951, all basic helicopter forms that had proved economically feasible had been developed and were in production. It was clear by 1951 that the helicopter would never replace the automobile as the primary means of civilian transportation. The helicopter's main civilian use would be to serve a relatively limited area of industry willing to pay the helicopter's costs. But the helicopter made great strides in the military market. Without military interest in the helicopter and the exigencies of the Cold War, helicopter design, expensive for the size of the market, may have languished at mid-1950 levels.

In 1948, a war to evict the British began in Malaya that would last until 1960. The British retaliated with tactics that included taking the fight to the insurgents. To supply their forces, the British relied heavily on helicopters to ferry troops in and carry wounded out. The helicopter proved its worth as a rescue vehicle.

But the Korean War really brought the helicopter to the attention of the world's military. General George E. Stratemyer, the first commander to use helicopters for medical evacuation, was the Far East Air Force Commander when the Korean War broke out. Almost immediately, he ordered the formation of special air evacuation units. He used six of the nine H-5 helicopters stationed in Japan and requested fourteen more from the United States and Europe.

The diminutive Bell H-13D Sioux, or HTL-4 (Marine Corps version), was also deployed to Korea but was quickly supplemented by Sikorsky's H-19 Chickasaw. This new helicopter, which first flew in November 1949, used a single main rotor and a vertical tail rotor. The H-19C was used widely in Korea. Techniques for ferrying troops into the assault, battlefield resupply, and rapid movement of heavy guns were all worked out under combat conditions.

In June 1950, the United States Marine Corps' experimental helicopter squadron HMX-1 supplied officers, men, and four HO3S-1 helicopters to Marine Observation Squadron VMO-6. Since VMO-6 was already flying fixed wing light aircraft, this helicopter addition made VMO-6 the first composite squadron. By August 1950, VMO-6 was in action near Pusan, Korea, and carried out reconnaissance, medical evacuation, logistics, liaison, artillery spotting, and rescue missions.

In 1951, the Marine Corps formed HMR-161, the first helicopter squadron devoted to transporting supplies. HMR-161 was equipped with

Top left: The U.S. Army's first helicopter was the R-4, developed from the VS-300, Igor Sikorsky's first successful helicopter. The R-4 entered service in 1944.

15 Sikorsky HRS-1s, the Marine Corps version of the Army's H-19 Chickasaw. The HRS-1 could carry 10 fully equipped combat soldiers. In September 1951, 12 helicopters from HMR-161 airlifted a 228-man company of combat Marines and nearly 10 tons of supplies to a hilltop 3,000 feet high, enabling the Marines to outflank a North Korean offensive. That "air assault" was the first in history made with a helicopter.

The Navy also made extensive use of helicopters during the Korean conflict. Helicopters served as plane guards for carriers and carried out search and rescue missions. And one Navy helicopter crew transformed their craft into a gunship when they fired pistols and carbines at North Korean troops during a rescue mission. A Navy HO3S-1 helicopter used a helicopter's unique flying abilities in the first attack on a helicopter by fixed wing fighters. Three MiG 15s fired on an HO3S-1 while it was rescuing South Korean soldiers. The pilot outmaneuvered the MiGs by flying very slow at tree level and hiding against the terrain. By the time the MiGs managed to turn, the helicopter had disappeared.

Army helicopter experiences largely mirrored those of the Marine Corps and the Navy. Army aviation had been defined by the 1947 National Security Act, which had limited the Army to fixed and rotary wing aircraft weighing 2,500 to 4,000 pounds. The Act also made the Army responsible for evacuation of battlefield casualties. But the Army looked beyond these restrictions and established a helicopter training facility at Fort Rucker, Alabama, in the late 1940s to train pilots and to develop new tactics involving the helicopter. A later agreement with the

Air Force rescinded the weight limits. The Army was permitted to transport supplies and troops within a defined combat zone.

The Army's first helicopters arrived in Korea in December 1950 and were used as artillery spotters and reconnaissance craft and to evacuate

Top: The Kaman H-43 Huskie has had a long and honorable career as the U.S. Air Force's basic fire fighter and rescue helicopter. **Bottom right:** A Marine Corps HRS-1 helicopter lands on the deck of the submarine USS *Sea Lion* in 1955 during an exercise in the Atlantic Ocean.

casualties. The first American helicopter—as distinct from its crew—to be armed belonged to the Army in 1951. It mounted a bazooka. But the Army's helicopter role in Korea was largely devoted to resupply and casualty evacuation. Army medevac helicopters flew 21,212 casualties to medical assistance. One major lesson learned from the Korean War was that specialized "ambulance" helicopters were not needed. All American military helicopters, no matter what their role, are designed to carry wounded soldiers.

Algeria: Birth of the Assault Helicopter

The Korean War ended inconclusively in 1953 in an armed truce. But 1953 also ushered in an era of limited wars. National liberation movements soon ringed the world. Some sought to replace colonial governments, some to establish communist governments, and many to do both. In 1954, the French-Indochina War ended in defeat for French colonial forces in Vietnam. A communist government was established in North Vietnam and a "democratic" government in South Vietnam. The helicopter saw only limited use by French forces in Vietnam.

At almost the same time the French wrenched themselves free of one colonial war in Indochina, they became involved in another against nationalist forces in Algeria. Algeria, located on the northern coast of the African continent, was a battleground particularly suited to the helicopter. Rising up from a narrow coastal plain, foothills roll up into a series of rugged mountains in the interior. There are few roads away from the coast, and these are easily blocked in the mountain passes.

At first, the French used the helicopter only to ferry equipment and supplies to units of the French Army operating in the interior. Gradually, helicopters began to carry troops into forward positions, and finally into battle. By 1959, there were some 200 helicopters operating in Algeria.

General George Grivas, the head of the *Ethniki Kyprion Agoniston* (National Organization of Cypriot Fighters), noted that when the British used helicopters to transport troops and supplies against his insurgents on Cyprus, they usually flew low and were vulnerable to well-aimed small arms fire. The unarmed helicopters were little physical threat to his fighters. The chief danger lay in the helicopter's ability to spot and report the movement of forces. Grivas also accurately forecast the major role helicopters would play in future insurgency wars when he described how they could be used in the assault role.

The French Army listened to Grivas. In 1957, when the French flew 56,000 hours of combat flights, six helicopters were hit by ground fire. By 1960, total flight hours had increased to more than 70,000, and no helicopters were hit. These results were achieved by arming helicopters and armoring them against small arms fire. The French also developed new tactics to deal with the fighter on the ground.

Outside the cities, the French Army emphasized mobile tactics. The Sikorsky OH-13, the H-19, the newer H-34, and the Vertol H-21 were

used, as was the Aerospatiale AS 313 Alouette II. Medical evacuation and cargo transport were the primary missions, but they were increasingly used as troop transports and assault weapons. The first use of an armed helicopter in Algeria involved a French Army unit that attacked Algerian resistance fighters entrenched in a strongly defended position in the Atala Mountains. The French commander placed two soldiers with automatic rifles in the litters mounted on either skid and drove the defenders from their position.

The French armed the H-21 Shawnee heavy-lift helicopter with two .30 caliber machine guns and 72 37 millimeter rockets. The Alouette II was armed with rockets only. The H-21s used by the French Navy had a swivel mount for a 20mm cannon. The SS-10 ground-to-ground anti-tank missile was also mounted on the armed helicopters. In 1956, the first air-to-ground missile, the SS-11, designed to be launched from a helicopter, was put into service. As the Algerian fighters had no heavy armor, these missiles were used mainly for destroying strongly defended areas.

As the French gained experience with helicopter tactics, they developed specific procedures. For instance, only one helicopter in six was heavily armed, and its sole task was to provide fire support while troops were being landed by other helicopters. French pilots were also instructed to make a straight-in approach as fast as possible to reduce the amount of time exposed to ground fire.

By the late 1950s, a typical assault mission involved a light fixed wing or rotary wing aircraft flying over the assault area a few minutes before the assault to report on the enemy's condition. Fixed wing aircraft heavily strafed the area just before the helicopters arrived and then stood off should their services be needed further. Armed helicopters flew in and saturated the immediate landing zone—invariably a hilltop—just before troop-carrying helicopters arrived. The transport helicopters dropped their troops and retired to a secondary landing zone nearby where more troops, brought up in ground vehicles, waited. These troops were also ferried forward. This task completed, the transport helicopters would move to a third secure landing zone should they be needed further. The French Army showed that helicopters, once considered too fragile for the assault role, were the ideal vehicle for moving and supporting troops quickly and in relative safety.

Vietnam

If the jeep was the all-purpose vehicle of World War II, then the helicopter served in the same capacity in Vietnam. Helicopters moved everything from troops to field guns, casualties to colonels. Understanding the terrain of South Vietnam helps explain the helicopter's impact on the war. In the north, the hills are high, rugged, and forested. They slide down to the central part of the country, which is low-lying farmland ending at the beaches of the South China Sea. In the west, the land jams

tened up a landing area. Other times, troops were airlifted into a zone without any prior strafing. Helicopter tactics were drastically upgraded. A combined pre-mission briefing was instituted that included the helicopter flight commander, the ground commander, fixed wing flight commander, and anyone else involved in the operation. Specialized helicopter units to provide armed escort for troop helicopters were also formed.

As the war expanded, the helicopter proved a useful tool on the battlefield. In response to the growing demand for more and more helicopters, the Secretary of Defense convened a board to study and recommend advances in Army air power. The board's report called for implementing a new doctrinal concept called "air mobility." The idea was to outflank and encircle enemy units by moving large numbers of troops by air rather than by ground. By September 1965, the 1st Cavalry (Airmobile) Division reached its base in South Vietnam.

The Marines went to Vietnam with substantially fewer helicopters than they had possessed at the end of the Korean War. In 1962, the Marine Corps had only about 220 UH-34D Choctaws, tired piston-engined helicopters capable of lifting less than 5,000 pounds each. In 1967, the Marines replaced the obsolete Choctaws with the gas turbine engine, single rotor CH-53A Sea Stallion. The Sea Stallion's payload was 18,500 pounds. In 1969, the Marines received the first real helicopter gunship, the Bell AH-1G HueyCobra. The HueyCobra set the design standard against which all future helicopter gunships would be measured.

The Air Force began search and rescue operations in January 1962. At first, the Kaman HH-43 Husky, a short-range aircraft, and the Sikorsky CH-3 were used. In November 1965, the Air Force received six Sikorsky HH-3Es, the famed Jolly Green Giant. Eventually, the Jollys could reach every area of North and South Vietnam. In 1967, the Air Force purchased modified versions of the Marine Corps CH-53, the HH-53C Super Jolly Green Giant. The Super Jolly was equipped with night vision devices in 1971, and night-time rescues became a normal mode of operation.

The first Navy helicopters arrived in South Vietnam in 1965 to support the coastal and inner waterway patrols. Naval helicopters flying in the South China Sea and the Gulf of Tonkin had the additional task of recording all surface craft activity they encountered. Although naval helicopters had a variety of roles during Vietnam, the primary mission was always search and rescue. Plucking a downed airman from anywhere in North Vietnam, including one pilot from Haiphong Harbor, came to be a routine operation.

United States military operations in South Vietnam ended in January 1973. But some U.S. helicopters remained in South Vietnam to support American government personnel who remained behind to advise the South Vietnamese. By the time American forces withdrew from combat in 1973, 19 different types of helicopters had been flown in Vietnam:

This page: Two CH-46 Sea Knights, brand-new to the war in South Vietnam in 1966, airlift supplies from an aircraft carrier in the South China Sea. These, and other Marine Sea Knights, were based at Marble Mountain Air Base near Da Nang.

up against the rugged, forested Laotian highlands and crumples into ridges. The Mekong River floods the great coastal plain of South Vietnam. From May to October, monsoons dump a hundred inches of rain over most of the country. Roads between major cities are poorly paved tracks and between villages often no more than footpaths.

The United States Army and Marine Corps moved into South Vietnam with the same helicopters the French had flown in Algeria. The UH-1 Huey was introduced in 1962 as a medevac helicopter. The Huey's gas turbine engine gave it superior speed and cargo capacity over piston-engined helicopters. With the start of American combat operations in 1964, the UH-1A was upgraded to the UH-1B by adding a more powerful engine and arming it with machine guns and rockets.

In the early stages of American involvement in the war, helicopter tactics were applied inconsistently. Sometimes fixed wing aircraft sof-

Cobras, HueyCobras, Shawnees, Sea Knights, Chinooks, Sea Stallions, Chickasaws, Huskies, Kiowas, Hueys, and many others.

Helicopter Development Since Vietnam

The helicopter as a battle weapon has been tested three times in major conflicts since the end of the Vietnam War. During the Falkland Islands War in 1982, the British learned the same lesson the United States learned in 1980 during the aborted Iran Hostage rescue mission. The mission in Iran failed not because of the fragility of helicopters but rather through a lack of proper staff work, communication, and preparation.

But the helicopter still more than proved its worth in the Falklands, where Great Britain fought Argentina for possession of these islands. As early in the conflict as April 21, British helicopters were engaged in ferrying Special Air Service commandos onto the Fortuna Glacier under the worst weather conditions imaginable. And when the weather finally tied the Special Air Service down, helicopters took them off again. On April 25, three different helicopters, a Wessex-3 Sea King, a Wasp, and a Lynx combined to attack, run aground, and finally sink the Argentinean submarine Santa Fe.

Various helicopters demonstrated the aircraft's versatility in many ways. After the HMS Sheffield was torpedoed on May 4, a Wasp served as an air ambulance, firefighter, ferry craft, and an antisubmarine helicopter all on the same day. A Lynx from the HMS Coventry sank an Argentinean patrol boat with an air-launched Sea Skua guided missile. On May

25, Sea Kings and a Wessex rescued survivors from the HMS Coventry, the HMS Broadsword, and the transport ship Atlantic Conveyor. The small British helicopter fleet also ferried troops, supplies, and equipment about the islands on an around-the-clock basis, as well as conducting reconnaissance and security patrols. While the British would have ultimately triumphed in the Falklands without the helicopter, the cost in lives and effort would have been far higher.

Operation Urgent Fury was a United States military assault in 1983 against the Marxist government on the Caribbean island of Grenada. It was the first vertical assault by American forces ever conducted from ships against an entrenched enemy. Helicopters from the Marine Corps HMM-261 Squadron were used to ferry in assault troops and reserves.

Both Army and Marine Corps helicopters were involved in every landing of assault forces during the campaign. Helicopters also provided all logistics and medevac support. A total of 107 military helicopters of 10 different types were involved. The U.S. Department of Defense stated that only four helicopters were lost to enemy ground fire: two AH-1T Sea Cobras, one CH-46E Sea Knight, and one UH-60A Blackhawk. Five other Blackhawks were severely damaged—three of them during the air assault on the Calivigny Barracks—but considered repairable.

The Grenadian operation raised again the question of the survivability of the helicopter on the modern battlefield. The only real antiaircraft equipment the Grenadian armed forces and their Cuban allies possessed was the ZSU-23 antiaircraft gun, which is a double-barreled, manually aimed and fired 23mm weapon. American forces encountered no portable antiaircraft missiles or radar-directed antiaircraft guns or guided missiles.

The Soviets were more than ever convinced of the utility of the assault helicopter after studying the American experience in the Vietnam War. In 1972, the first version of the Soviet Mi-24 (NATO codenamed Hind) was flown. The Hind was built as an assault helicopter that provided its own covering fire to clear a landing zone. It is a fast helicopter and is normally armed with a machine gun or a cannon. The Hind endured a thorough shakedown in Afghanistan. The Afghan terrain, mostly high mountains and rugged valleys with few roads, is ideal country for the helicopter. By 1983, the Soviets had deployed more than 600 helicopters in Afghanistan to support their own and Afghan government forces. Soviet helicopter tactics in Afghanistan were similar to those used by the United States in Vietnam and the French in Algeria.

The Soviets gained valuable helicopter experience, but they did not have it all their own way. Afghan resistance fighters learned to ambush helicopters in the high mountain passes. They used heavy machine guns to direct concentrated fire against those helicopter parts vulnerable to small arms fire—the engine compartment, rotor hubs, and cockpit. Still, the helicopters made it difficult for the resistance troops to move effectively by day.

Top left: A Sikorsky Sea King helicopter lifts a load of ammunition from the deck of the HMS Hermes during the Falkland Islands War in 1982.

In 1985, the United States and Great Britain began to supply Stinger and Blowpipe portable antiaircraft missiles to the Afghan resistance fighters. Within weeks, the complexion of the air war changed. Soviet helicopters—transport and assault craft alike—were forced to fly either so high that surveillance of the countryside suffered or so low the helicopter became vulnerable to small arms fire. Close support of ground forces also had to be withdrawn at times when helicopter casualties became too great.

Soviet pilots in Afghanistan evolved tactics and maneuvers that lessened, but did not end, the missile threat. Flare dispensers were fitted to Soviet aircraft of all types. When the pilot thought he detected a missile threat, flares were strewn in the aircraft's flight path to decoy the missile. Pilots also began flying higher than the missile could reach and performing more night operations.

The Stinger missile is credited by knowledgeable sources with having a great deal to do with the Soviet decision to withdraw from Afghanistan. In 1987, the Stinger alone successfully killed its target 58 percent of the time. By the time the Soviets withdrew in 1989, they had lost nearly 1,000 aircraft. Helicopters accounted for 80 percent of those loses, 200 or more of which were Mi-24 Hinds. But the helicopter remains a major battlefield threat. This is borne out by the Soviet's Operation Kunarski in 1985. The Soviets dropped 11,000 troops into a battle zone without losing a single helicopter.

The Helicopter Today

The United States military spent hundreds of thousands of hours evaluating the wartime use of the helicopter during the Vietnam War. The U.S. military also assessed the Soviet experience in Afghanistan, as well as helicopter experience gained in Iran, the Falklands, and Grenada. The consensus among the world's military forces is that the helicopter remains an indispensable part of military operations, but it must be used with care and with regard for the type and kind of antiaircraft measures an enemy will take against it. Grenada and the Falklands both demonstrated conclusively that a thorough understanding of the conflict and the enemy's resources, dispositions, and morale is vital. A well thought out, well rehearsed use plan is also essential.

The result of recent helicopter evaluation is a new generation of assault helicopters now on the drawing boards or entering military service. One spur in the West has been the development of the tank as the preeminent weapon of war in central Europe. The main battle tank (MBT) today is so heavily armored and armed that it is all but impervious to currently issued portable antitank weapons. The MBT's fire control system enables it to deal with other MBTs on an equal basis or with soft-armored vehicles like the TOW missile-equipped M2 Bradley Cavalry Vehicle. The tank's heavy machine guns are effective against soft-skinned vehicles like the Soviet BMP-1, which is equipped with the SS-3 Sagger.

Today, mobile, radar-guided antiaircraft guns and missiles have made it too risky for any but the most specialized fixed wing aircraft to attempt to engage armored formations. That job has passed to the helicopter. The French were the first to recognize the unique capabilities of the helicopter as an antitank weapon. In the early 1950s, the French developed the first *helicopters anti-chars,* or antitank helicopters. These were Alouette IIs armed with SS-10 wire-guided missiles. The operator had to guide the missile to its target, which was no mean feat in a vibrating, shifting helicopter.

This manual command guidance system has given way to more sophisticated systems represented by such missiles as the TOW or Hellshot. As the tank threat grows, the clamor for antitank helicopters grows as well. But the development of new weapons systems has become so expensive that the present generation of helicopters dedicated to antitank warfare is represented only by the Agusta 129 Mongoose, the AH-64H Apache, and the AH-1W SuperCobra. All three are attack helicopters designed specifically for the anti-armor role.

Today, most helicopters designed for battlefield use have some antitank capability. Helicopters that are not equipped to carry laser-guided missiles can "pop up" from cover, lock their aiming sensors on their

This page: Members of 40 Commando, Royal Marines, board a Wessex V helicopter while taking part in Display Determination exercises in 1983.

target, and then fire and guide their missiles home. The main drawback to this technique is that the helicopter is exposed to enemy fire for a longer period of time. But if several helicopters attack an enemy armored force with coordinated efforts, this method can be very effective.

A second spur to helicopter development has been the rise of the electronic battlefield. As military forces around the world have become increasingly sophisticated, the battlefield has become more lethal and therefore more inaccessible. The helicopter offers a way to meet and defeat both the threat of radar-guided antiaircraft weapons and missiles as well as concentrations of heavily defended logistic, communication, and command centers, and troop concentrations.

The World War II concept of the scout helicopter has taken on new meaning. Small, agile helicopters are equipped with sophisticated electronics mounted on their cockpit roofs or at the top of their rotor masts. They can edge in toward enemy positions while using natural terrain and vegetation, as well as buildings, for cover. The scout helicopters can then either direct more heavily armed helicopters to the target or fire their own weaponry.

When the United States Navy was deployed to the Persian Gulf in 1987–88 to protect neutral shipping from Iranian and Iraqi air and gunboat attacks, 15 OH-58B Kiowa helicopters were fitted with Hellfire air-to-ground missiles, .50 caliber machine guns, and 2.75-inch rockets. Termed AHIP (Army Helicopter Improvement Program), these Kiowas were quite successful. Although no firm numbers have yet been published, it is known that the Kiowas damaged and sank numerous gunboats that fired on them or on neutral shipping. The AHIP was intended to serve as a temporary scout and attack helicopter until the LHX (Light Helicopter Experimental) design became available in the late 1990s. But federal budget considerations forced extensive cutbacks, and only 207 of the modified OH-58D Kiowas have been purchased.

The Soviet Union has the most extensive helicopter force in service today. In Europe, before the proposed cutback in Warsaw Pact/NATO forces went into effect, the Soviets deployed as many as 20 attack regiments. Most of those helicopters are now equipped with infrared jammers, flares, and additional armor in response to the lessons of Afghanistan. And waiting in the wings is the Mi-28 (NATO codenamed Havoc), a new Soviet attack helicopter that will replace the Mi-24 Hind. A second new Soviet helicopter has been expressly designed for air-to-air combat against other helicopters. NATO codenamed Hokum, it is expected to enter service in the early 1990s.

Helicopter Technology

Helicopters fly because their rotor blades accelerate a column of air downward that weighs more than the craft. This produces a reaction that pushes the helicopter upward. The explanation sounds simple, but the practice is extremely complicated.

Airfoils

Although they look very different, fixed wing and rotary wing aircraft share the same basic principle of flight. Two forces work together to lift an aircraft. The first force develops when a wing meets at an angle the airstream moving toward it. The airstream presses against the bottom of the wing, and the wing presses back. As much as 15 percent of the total force required to lift an aircraft is supplied by this force. The second force derives from the fact that when air flows over a curved surface, it becomes less dense. For that reason, aircraft wings are curved across their tops but left relatively flat along their bottom surfaces.

When the airstream meets the wing, the airstream splits. The air that flows across the top of the wing travels faster than the air flowing along the bottom. The air flowing faster across the top becomes less dense than the air moving along the bottom at a slower rate. The denser air beneath the wing pushes upward, seeking to expand into the area where the air is less dense. The difference in air pressure between the top and bottom of the wing produces most of the force needed to lift the aircraft. A difference of 2.5 ounces of air pressure per square inch will provide 20 pounds of lifting force to each square foot of wing surface.

A helicopter's wing is its main rotor. Each blade, although considerably narrower than an airplane's fixed wing, is curved much like an airplane wing. To obtain lift, the rotor blade is angled to a greater degree than a fixed wing. The two lifting forces act on the blade. The airstream moving toward the blade pushes on it, and the blade pushes back, producing a small amount of lift. Then, as the air flows faster across the top than the bottom of the blade, denser air beneath the blade seeks to expand into the low-pressure area created above the blade, pushing the blade upward.

Short, stubby wings can be found on some helicopters, most notably the Soviet Mi-24 gunship. The wings provide an extra lift surface, helping to reduce the amount of weight the main rotor must lift. The wings also increase speed and cruising range. In helicopters intended for military duty, they serve as additional attachment points for weaponry.

But the similarity between fixed wing and rotary wing aircraft largely ends at this point. The fixed wing aircraft is a relatively stable platform once airborne. By adjusting the control surfaces on the wings and horizontal and vertical stabilizer, the fixed wing aircraft will fly a relatively straight and level course. Not so the helicopter. While each rotor blade is generating lift, the rotor system as a whole is pulling a vast amount of air down and through itself. When the weight of that air exceeds the weight of the helicopter minus the lift generated, the helicopter rises. As the helicopter rises, it must balance on the column of air its main rotor has produced. Imagine balancing a long pole on one hand; this will give some idea of the instability involved. To overcome that instability, two controls are used: the collective pitch and the cyclic pitch.

The Collective Pitch

The pilot controls the rate at which the helicopter rises by tilting the main rotor blades along their horizontal axis so that they cut through the air at a greater or lesser angle—called pitch—to pull more or less air through the rotor system. As the pilot starts his takeoff, his left hand pulls up on a lever—the collective pitch—located on the left side of the seat. This lever controls the angle, or pitch, of all the blades at the same time. The steeper the blade angle (up to a point), the more lift is generated and the more air is pushed down. The term "collective" is used because the lever causes the pitch of all blades in the rotor system to change at the same time.

As long as the pilot keeps the blades set at the same angle he used for takeoff, the helicopter will continue to rise. To achieve forward flight, energy must be exerted along the horizontal axis of the helicopter. One way to accomplish this is to add another engine to pull or push the craft forward. But this method adds weight and reduces the system's efficiency. A better way is to use the blade system itself. If the blade system can be tipped forward, then air in front of, rather than above, the helicopter will be pulled through the blades.

The Cyclic Pitch

To move the helicopter forward, the pilot pushes another lever, called the cyclic and usually mounted between his knees, in the direction he wishes to go. This lever tilts the main rotor blades in that direction. The blades are now pulling air down through the rotor from both in front of as well as above the craft, providing both lift and forward propulsion. But, as with everything connected with a helicopter, just tilting the main rotor system on its shaft will not satisfy the requirements of forward motion.

To enable the massive main rotor and its shaft to tilt in any direction would impose a terrible weight penalty, making the helicopter far too cumbersome. Instead, the helicopter's main rotor is attached to a series of hinges, which in turn are connected to the rigid central shaft rotated by the engine. Each rotor blade is attached to a circular hub called the "upper swash plate." It in turn rides on the "lower swash plate," which is a triangular plate attached to three hydraulic actuators. The hydraulic actuators tilt the lower swash plate in response to the cyclic.

If the pilot pulls up on the cyclic control, a series of levers tilts the back side of the lower swash plate upward and lowers the front side. The upper swash plate follows. Each rotor blade in turn moves downward as it approaches the front of its circular path and upward again as it reaches the back. In effect, the main rotor assembly has been tipped in the direction the pilot wishes to move.

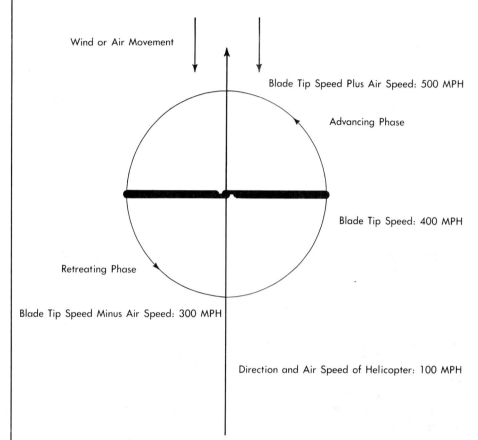

Wind or Air Movement

Blade Tip Speed Plus Air Speed: 500 MPH

Advancing Phase

Blade Tip Speed: 400 MPH

Retreating Phase

Blade Tip Speed Minus Air Speed: 300 MPH

Direction and Air Speed of Helicopter: 100 MPH

Helicopter Blade: Advancing and Retreating Phases

Blade Tip Speed Versus Flying Speed

As complicated as the explanations for the two major control processes are, it gets more complicated still. The individual blade tips of the main rotor system move at different speeds, depending on where in the circular path the blade tips are. When the helicopter hovers, the blade tips all move at the same speed because air is being pulled down through the rotor system from above. When the pilot uses the cyclic lever to tilt the main rotor, each blade tip cuts *across* the airstream. Thus, each blade tip moves at different speeds relative to the direction of flight.

Look down on an imaginary two-bladed helicopter rotor from above with the blades at the 3 and 9 o'clock positions. When the helicopter is hovering, both blade tips will be moving in a counterclockwise circle at, say, 400 miles per hour. The blade at the 3 o'clock position is in the advancing phase since it is moving toward the airstream while the blade at 9 o'clock is in the retreating phase, moving away from the airstream. Now, let the helicopter move forward at 100 miles per hour. The air speed of the tip of the 3 o'clock blade is the sum of the speed of rotation

(400 miles per hour) plus the forward speed of the helicopter (100 miles per hour), or 500 miles per hour. The air speed of the blade tip at the 9 o'clock position is the speed of rotation (400 miles per hour) minus the forward speed of the helicopter (100 miles per hour), or 300 miles per hour.

If the helicopter's forward speed increased to 350 miles per hour, the air speed of the blade tip in the advancing phase (3 o'clock position) will approach the speed of sound. The blade in the retreating phase (9 o'clock position), meanwhile, will have slowed to 50 miles per hour. Sonic shock effects will act on the advancing blade, while the retreating blade will approach a stall condition in which it produces no lift. With no lift from the retreating blades, the entire helicopter will roll out of control. This is why helicopters using a conventional blade system on the main rotor will probably never fly much faster than 300 miles per hour.

Torque

Torque is a major factor to be considered in helicopters whose rotors are driven by an engine acting through a drive shaft. The spinning of the drive shaft produces "torque," or twist, that acts in the direction the blades are spinning. Torque spins the body of the helicopter in the opposite direction of the blades. Unless counteracted, the helicopter's fuselage will rotate uncontrollably.

Several systems have been tried to combat torque; the most common today is the tail rotor. The tail rotor spins vertically, like a propeller on a fixed wing aircraft, and uses the tail boom as a lever to force the tail in the opposite direction of spin imparted by the main rotor's torque. The pitch of the tail rotor's blades can usually be varied to produce more or less thrust as needed.

Rotor Designs

There are five basic configurations of main and tail rotor designs that have developed over the years. The most common is the familiar main tail and rotor (MTR) configuration: a large main rotor provides lift and horizontal motion, and a small tail rotor offsets the torque produced by the main rotor. Probably 80 percent of all helicopters flying today use this system.

The second most widely used configuration is the tandem rotor system. Two large rotors are used; one is located at the fore of the craft's fuselage, the other aft. The two blade systems rotate in opposition to one another and are timed to intermesh at any speed. The opposing rotation cancels out the torque produced by either engine.

A third rotor design, the "eggbeater" system, has never been widely employed. The design was used by Kaman in their famous HH-43 Husky series as well as by the Kamov design bureau for their series of Soviet naval helicopters. In this system, two sets of blades are mounted on separate but side by side shafts. The blades are set at an angle to the horizontal plane of the helicopter. A set of intermeshing gears assures that the blades always turn in opposition to one another, thus canceling the torque effect each produces.

The World War II German Focke Achgelis Fa 223 Drach, the first helicopter to enter regular production, and the post-World War II Soviet Mi-12 helicopter, designed by the Mil bureau (founded by Mikhail Mil but currently headed by Marat N. Tishchenko), are two of the few helicopter designs using the fourth rotor configuration, twin side-by-side rotors. The Mi-12 and the Fa 223 used two sets of rotors mounted outboard of the fuselage. The rotors turned opposite to one another and intermeshed. Unlike the eggbeater system used in the Husky, however, these rotors revolved in a horizontal plane. The Mi-12, designed as a heavy-lift helicopter for the vast reaches of Siberia, never entered production. The Bell Textron V-22 "tilt rotor" aircraft uses a similar system but only during the ascent/descent phase of its flight. The V-22 is discussed in detail in the United States helicopter profiles.

The fifth rotor design system is the twin coaxial arrangement. Two rotor systems, one above the other, turn in opposite directions, eliminating torque problems. This system is very compact and was used by the Soviet Kamov designers for a series of antisubmarine warfare (ASW) helicopters.

Other rotor systems have been widely investigated with a view to improving the helicopter's performance and speed. Perhaps the most promising is the advancing blade concept (ABC) in which twin, counter-rotating rigid blades are used. A helicopter blade provides maximum lift as it begins its advancing phase (the 3 o'clock position) and the least lift in the retreating phase (the 9 o'clock position). With the ABC design, one counter-rotating blade enters the advancing phase as the other enters the retreating phase. Since one blade is always advancing, the helicopter has maximum lift and speed at all times. It is thought that the new Soviet anti-air helicopter, code-named Hokum by NATO, employs the ABC concept.

Several successful helicopters were built using main rotor blades turned by gas turbine engine exhaust directed through the main rotor blade tips. This system had the advantages of low torque—only that produced by friction on the rotor bearings—and low infrared radiation since the exhaust was cooled almost immediately by the rotor wash. The major disadvantage was high fuel consumption.

A final system of note is the no tail rotor (NOTAR) design most recently tested by McDonnell Douglas Helicopter Company. The NOTAR design eliminates the need for a tail rotor. Instead, compressed air is forced through a slit in the tail boom to counteract main rotor torque. Eliminating the tail rotor has the advantage of reducing complexity and noise. The NOTAR rotor concept was first tried in the British Cierva W-9 helicopter as early as 1946.

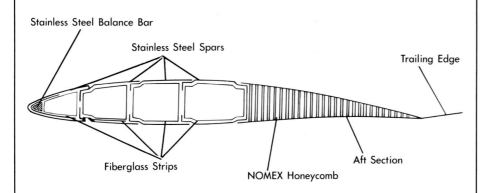

Stainless Steel Balance Bar
Stainless Steel Spars
Trailing Edge
Fiberglass Strips
NOMEX Honeycomb
Aft Section

Rotor Blades

The helicopter's blades are possibly the most heavily stressed part of the helicopter. While turning, they are subject to a wide variety of horizontal and vertical stresses including a flapping movement induced while passing from advancing to retreating phases and back again. Blades made of solid materials, such as aluminum or steel, are heavy and subject to metal fatigue.

Today's helicopter blades are marvels of engineering, combining plastics, foams, glass fibers, and exotic metals. The blades used in the United States Army's CH-47 Chinook are typical. The interior leading edge of the blade is formed from a metal rod with a D-shaped cross section and is covered with glass fiber skin. The interior trailing edge is made of a metal honeycomb material. The whole exterior of the blade is covered with titanium sheeting for added strength and to prevent pitting and erosion caused by airborne dirt.

Bell Textron's high-technology blade for its 412 model uses a polymer honeycomb and a fiberglass and carbon leading edge reinforced with carbon fiber spars that run the length of the blade. A titanium covering on the leading edge adds strength and can cut through unexpected obstacles like power wires—the leading cause of helicopter crashes—or tree branches.

The United States Army's AH-64A Apache main rotor blades are made of stainless steel spars and fiberglass tubes arranged in a box cross section. This makes for an exceptionally strong blade that can shrug off hits from .50 caliber machine guns or 23 millimeter high-explosive shells or cut through tree branches up to two inches in diameter.

Rotor Hub

The rotor hub is probably the most delicate structure aboard a helicopter and the one most exposed to potential damage, especially in combat. The center point of the rotor assembly is the rotor hub, which is attached to the drive shaft. The blades are fitted to the hub through a series of hinges that permit the blades to flap up and down. In most helicopter rotor systems, the hinges are steel or other high-strength metals, such as titanium. But materials technology is beginning to supply plastics that do the job with less fatigue, greater strength, and reduced vibration.

A typical rotor hub has roots to which the blades are attached. The root is attached to the hub by a flapping hinge that allows the blade to move up and down. A pitch arm is attached to each root to control the blade's angle of attack (the angle at which the blade meets the air). A linkage connected to each pitch arm supplies the mechanical force to twist the pitch arm/blade combination. The pitch arm in turn is attached to the lower swash plate. This entire hub assembly rides on the upper swash plate, which rotates above the fixed lower swash plate. The tilt, or pitch, of the lower swash plate is controlled by the action of either mechanical or hydraulic servomechanisms that move the lower swash plate in the desired direction. As the speed, weight, and complexity of a helicopter increases, so does the complexity of the hub assembly.

Airframes and Armor

The helicopter is basically an inefficient means of flying. It consumes a vast amount of power compared with a fixed wing aircraft—a helicopter

Rotor Hub Assembly

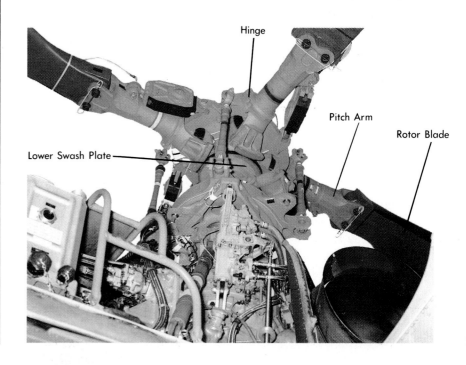

Hinge
Pitch Arm
Rotor Blade
Lower Swash Plate

Top left: The rotor blade is a helicopter's "wing." Modern rotor blades are complex pieces of machinery composed of many different parts. **Bottom right:** The modern helicopter's main rotor blade system is extremely sophisticated. For the helicopter to fly and maneuver properly, all the various components have to work in near-perfect synchronization.

21

requires the same energy output as a fixed wing aircraft to fly one-third the distance with one-third the payload. Thus, a helicopter's airframe must be light yet sturdy. Usually, the airframe is built from hollow metal tubing that is reinforced in all such load-bearing areas as the engine and the main and tail rotor mounts. The tubing is then covered with a tightly fitted metal skin that helps hold the airframe together and maintain its rigid shape. This type of structure is referred to as a monocoque fuselage.

Fuselage coverings can range from nothing, as in the early Bell H-13, to the composite carbon fiber skin panels used in today's Sikorsky S-75. The venerable H-13 had an open framework and a plexiglass bubble enclosing the cockpit. The Piasecki HRP-1 Rescuer (also called the Flying Banana) was covered with fabric, as were the Sikorsky R-4 and the German Focke Achgelis Fa 223 Drach of pre-World War II design, the world's first production helicopter. The majority of helicopters flying today use aluminum covering, either as paneling or as part of a foam or honeycomb sandwich, to provide additional strength and rigidity to the frame. Steel and titanium are often used for reinforcement, particularly for the cargo decks and ramps in such transport helicopters as the United States Air Force HH-53 Super Jolly Green Giant.

Rolled steel is used for armor plating to protect crew members and such vital parts of the aircraft as the rotor masts and the areas around the engine compressor and turbine blades. The United States Marine Corps uses hinged steel panels in their CH-46 Sea Knight to provide crew protection against small arms fire. But increasingly, for small arms protection, steel is giving way to lighter high-technology materials like Kevlar. Unfortunately, helicopters are so inherently fragile and vulnerable that there seems no way of armoring them against anything larger than .50 caliber or 23mm high-explosive rounds without incurring severe weight penalties.

Helicopter Engines

The successful development of the helicopter, even more so than the fixed wing aircraft, depended on the development of a lightweight engine. Even Leonardo da Vinci may have recognized this fact. While he attempted to build working models of most of his other inventions, there is no evidence da Vinci did so for his human-powered flying machine. Thomas A. Edison, following a serious accident with an electrically powered helicopter of his own design at the turn of the century, stated, "When an engine could be made that would weigh only three or four pounds to the horsepower, the problems of the air could be solved."

Today, Edison's requirements have been exceeded, with the latest engines providing weight-to-horsepower ratios in the range of 0.2 to 0.6. New varieties of engines, such as the Pratt & Whitney T800, will better those ratios.

Progressing from bow-and-string-powered rotors in 1784 through steam and gun cotton engines in the mid-1800s, powered, manned

flight by a helicopter was finally achieved four years after the Wright brothers flew their craft on the windswept beach at Kitty Hawk, North Carolina. In 1907, the four rotor Breguet-Richet No. 1 achieved an altitude of three feet, although it remained tethered and had to be steadied by handlers. A few weeks later, Paul Corneau's twin rotor design, powered by a 24-horsepower gasoline engine, achieved a few seconds of free flight. The age of the man-carrying helicopter had arrived.

But the success of fixed wing aircraft slowed helicopter development. Aviation enthusiasts were preoccupied with the heady thrills of flight. A new frontier was waiting to be explored, and few had time to waste on the complicated mechanisms and expensive development needed for vertical flight. During this period, internal combustion engine development continued, and when helicopter development began again in earnest after World War I, new lightweight engines were available. Development could now be concentrated on solving the myriad control problems associated with vertical flight.

Throughout the 1940s and 1950s, helicopter designers used gas reciprocating engines—the majority built in the West used either the reliable Pratt & Whitney Wasp series or licensed variations thereof that produced between 400 and 1,600 horsepower. But almost as soon as the new lightweight piston engines had made the helicopter an economic and practical reality, studies began to substitute an even lighter (in terms of horsepower produced per pound of engine) power plant, the gas turbine engine.

Design engineers quickly realized that if the far simpler gas turbine engine could be substituted for the gas piston engine, a host of complicated ancillary equipment (e.g., gear boxes, clutches, and cooling systems) could be eliminated. Gas turbine engines were also far more reliable and could run for longer periods without overhaul than gas

This page: This cutaway illustrates the General Electric T700 turboshaft engines that power the Sikorsky UH-60 Black Hawk.

piston engines. Gas turbine engines also burned a wide variety of fuels that were much less volatile than gasoline.

A gas turbine engine works by compressing great amounts of air and mixing that air with fuel to burn inside a combustion chamber. As the exhaust gases leave the combustion chamber (also called a burner can), they flow over and spin the turbine—a wheel covered with a curved set of vanes. The turbine is connected by a shaft to the air compressor, which is mounted *ahead* of the combustion chamber. The air compressor is also a vaned wheel, but these vanes are angled to compress the air before it enters the combustion chamber. When the turbine spins, the air compressor revolves, sending compressed air into the combustion chamber. Most gas turbine engines used in helicopters are turboshaft engines. In this type of engine, the exhaust gases turn a shaft, which turns the main and tail rotors through a series of gears.

Anything that increases the amount of air compressed or raises the temperature of the burning gases will increase the gas turbine engine's efficiency. Such efficiency increases, however, have to be balanced against fuel consumption and increasing complexity.

In the early days of rotary flight, all that was desired of an engine, piston or gas turbine, was that it be both light and powerful enough to lift the helicopter. As helicopter flight developed, the desirability of a second engine became obvious. Despite claims made for the inherent safety of a helicopter due to its ability to autorotate, i.e., descend at a controlled rate by allowing its main rotors to spin freely, a second engine was desirable for safety and extra power.

Gas piston engines were too heavy for most dual installations but as gas turbine technology developed, gas turbine engines grew lighter and lighter relative to horsepower produced. One of the first multiengined helicopters was the Soviet Mi-6, which first flew in 1957. It was powered by two 5,500 horsepower Soloviev D-25V turboshaft engines. The French Aerospatiale SA 321 Super Frelon, built in 1962, employed three turboshaft engines, each delivering 1,550 horsepower.

When operating over the ocean, two engines are especially desirable. The Soviet Kamov Ka-25, used for antisubmarine work, was designed with two turboshaft engines and first flew in 1960. At the same time, Pratt & Whitney, a division of United Technologies and one of the world's foremost producers of piston and gas turbine engines, took a somewhat different approach. Its PT6T turboshaft engine, designed at the East Hartford, Connecticut, plant and built at Pratt & Whitney Canada, has two engines driving a single transmission. Both engines normally work together at reduced power, but if one fails, the other increases its output to compensate.

Cockpit Design

The most important consideration in the design of a helicopter cockpit is providing the pilot with as much unobstructed visibility in all direc-

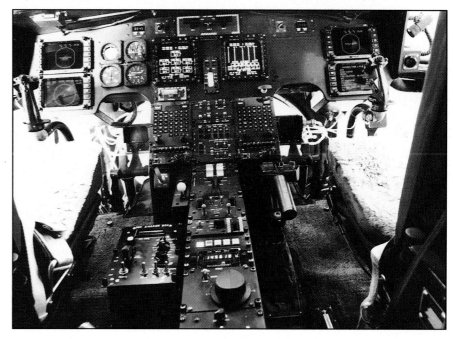

Top right: In older helicopters, the control and instrument panel was littered with dials, gauges, and indicators that required a great deal of the pilot's attention to monitor all systems. Lower right: In modern helicopters, pilot workload has been reduced through the introduction of video displays and various self-monitoring systems that eliminate the need for constant checking.

tions as possible. Helicopters are hard to fly, quite slow, and for the most part fly relatively close to the ground. To enhance survival in combat, pilots prefer to look outside the cockpit at all times. Therefore, controls and instrumentation must be as few in number as possible and placed within easy reach. The need for high visibility combined with minimum operating distraction presents a thorough challenge to designers.

Although helicopters have grown larger and more complicated over the years, modern electronics have made the cockpit simpler in layout.

Compare the photographs of the instrument panel of the SH-3 Sea King with that of the Boeing Model 360 Advanced Technology Helicopter. Even though the instrument groups are clustered for easy use, the Sea King's cockpit is still a maze of switches and analogue dials that require the pilot to focus on each one to read it. Now glance at the Model 360 control panel. All units are dominated by video display screens that present the pilot with only the information he needs to know to fly the aircraft.

During the 1990s, helicopter cockpit control panels will move toward computerized multifunction video monitors. These displays will replace separate analogue and digital instruments. Information will be presented to the pilot in the order of "most frequently" to "least frequently" needed, or most critical to most routine. By touching a switch or speaking a command, the display will be able to change from horizon indication to engine temperature to altitude to air and/or ground speed to weapons status. This information could be displayed on a monitor placed in the instrument panel or even in a shortened form on the faceplate of the pilot's helmet.

Flying a helicopter is a full-time job. There is rarely time to relax and sightsee when at the controls. In combat, the situation is even more difficult. The pilot must search both the ground over which he is flying and the sky around him for enemy threats. Night flying creates even greater demands. Military pilots wear night-vision goggles that provide an enhanced display outside the cockpit but have several drawbacks. Night-vision goggles are essentially two television cameras mounted side by side. Thus, they do not provide great depth-of-field vision, and they restrict peripheral vision to a 60 degree field. Despite manufacturers' claims, current state-of-the-art night-vision devices do not adjust instantly between the brighter ambient light outside a cockpit and the dimmer light inside. For varying, if short, periods of time, the pilot's vision is obscured should he shift vision quickly from outside to inside. Thus, the simpler a helicopter cockpit is arranged and the fewer switches and instruments to be adjusted and turned, the more efficient the pilot can be.

This leads to a second question in helicopter cockpit design: how many crew members should there be in the cockpit? From a personnel standpoint, the answer is one. Smaller countries with declining or static populations are finding it increasingly difficult to recruit sufficient qualified personnel for military service. The problem is especially acute with respect to flying personnel.

To gain an appreciation of how busy a helicopter pilot is during flight, let's look briefly at the pilot of an attack helicopter flying a mission.

At the pre-mission briefing, the pilot is given his objective. From this he plans his weapons load and his flight path in and out of the combat zone. He also surveys current intelligence for the type and nature of threats affecting his helicopter. Weather information is taken into account. Once in the air, he must fly the helicopter while paying close attention to altitude and speed, engine temperature and revolutions, and any warning lights signaling a malfunction. If he is flying with other helicopters, he must watch his own station keeping (position), as well as that of his wingmen. As he nears the combat zone, the pilot must search the ground for enemy troops equipped with antiaircraft guns or missiles. This involves watching for telltale smoke trails (tracers) or antiaircraft rockets rising from vegetated areas, camouflaged gun emplacements, and enemy troops or vehicles. During the flight, he must also monitor the radio frequencies being used by the air controllers. If he is leading the strike, he is responsible for tactical communication and navigation. If he is not leading the strike, he must still monitor the flight plan.

Once over the combat zone, the pilot must find the targets, select weapons, and aim and fire them. At the same time, he must be constantly aware of enemy countermeasures. As experience in Vietnam and Afghanistan has shown, ground forces quickly become sophisticated in antihelicopter tactics. These days, the pilot must dispense antiaircraft flares to decoy enemy ground-to-air missiles using infrared detectors. The pilot must also drop chaff to confuse enemy radar-guided missiles. These electronic countermeasures are as much art as technical procedure. And at all times, the pilot must be taking, or be ready to take, violent evasive action.

This brief overview of a modern helicopter combat mission gives some idea of how busy a military helicopter pilot can be. The pilots of large transport helicopters like the United States Marine Corps CH-53E Sea Stallion are scarcely less busy as they fly long transport routes with few if any civilian navigational aids. And these pilots must be even more attentive to ground threats because they generally have only door-mounted .50 caliber machine guns and flares and chaff to defend themselves.

So, despite a growing shortage of qualified people to flesh out flight crews, two in the cockpit is considered the ideal number so that navigational, threat monitoring, and weapons handling tasks can be shared.

Modern military helicopter cockpits are arranged in one of two ways: 1) side-by-side seating, in which the pilot and copilot/weapons operator sit side by side and 2) in tandem, in which the pilot and copilot/weapons operator sit one behind the other. In the latter arrangement, the pilot usually sits behind and above the copilot/weapons officer for better all-round vision.

The copilot/weapons officer is usually equipped with numerous vision aides—radar, infrared and light-enhancing image intensifiers, and aiming devices—to increase the efficiency of his weaponry. The weapons officer is also usually a fully qualified copilot. His section of the cockpit comes equipped with duplicate controls so he can fly and fight should the pilot be injured or killed. The pilot also has duplicates of some weapon controls for the same reason.

There are advantages and disadvantages to both seating arrangements. Advocates of side-by-side seating stress the psychological benefits, especially in combat situations, of having a partner beside you. They also emphasize improved communications via hand signals and the almost telepathic communication bond that can develop between a pilot and copilot after lengthy association.

The advocates of tandem seating point out that the helicopter can be made narrower, making it a harder target to hit. The side-by-side UH-1 Huey is 9.7 feet wide, while the tandem AH-64A Apache is only 3.16 feet wide. They also point out that higher levels of crew protection at a smaller weight penalty can be achieved in a tandem arrangement than in a side-by-side arrangement. Apache crew members are protected below and on each side by lightweight boron armor shields. Between pilot and copilot/weapons operator is a transparent Kevlar blast shield. Such protection is possible because the two crew members are isolated and protected individually. In a side-by-side helicopter, the entire cockpit would have to be armored, including the dead space between the seats.

Tandem helicopters are usually longer than side-by-side helicopters, which imposes a weight penalty due to a longer tail boom and supporting structure. When coupled with the higher cockpit required by elevated seating, the performance characteristics of the aircraft are altered. But tandem advocates point out that a tandem seater is more streamlined, which increases speed. Side-by-side advocates counter that streamlining requires more engine power when decelerating, which means greater engine noise and less agility for maneuvering.

Visibility is another element much debated. Tandem advocates note that in side-by-side seating arrangements, the pilot tends to maneuver in the direction in which he has the best visibility. The Viet Cong and the Afghan resistance fighters demonstrated that that point is quickly learned. The elevated pilot's seat provides the pilot with a far better view in all directions, but side-by-side proponents argue that two crew members have smaller areas to watch, and therefore can "see" better. Obviously, there are no easy answers to the question of seating arrangements.

Visual and Optical Control Systems

Technology has progressed the fastest during the past decade in the area of visual and optical control systems. The helicopter crew member of today has a range of visual aids extending from infrared sensors to sophisticated helmet head-up-displays (HUD).

In a head-up-display, the helmet's faceplate is imprinted with a liquid crystal display similar to the screen of a pocket calculator. Portions of the display become visible when an electric current causes the liquid crystals to darken or change color. The crew member's helmet is plugged into the same information-handling system that feeds the traditional instrumentation on his control panel. Edited versions of the information the pilot

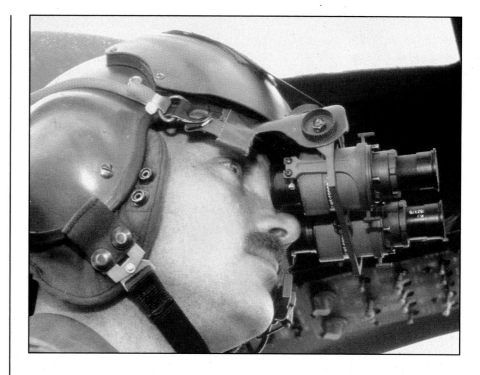

needs to know to fly and fight his aircraft are shown on the HUD. Thus, the pilot only needs to refocus his eyes to read such data as altitude, air and ground speed, heading, weapons status, and air or ground threats that have been detected by his radar. At the same time, through his peripheral vision, he remains aware of what is happening beyond the cockpit.

Taking the HUD one step further, extensive research and development has been conducted over the past decade on completely artificial visual systems. The pilot wears a special helmet that encloses his head. He "sees" a series of computer-generated images representing his flight path, most commonly as a three dimensional routing to the target. Enemy defensive areas are highlighted and enemy antiaircraft systems are pinpointed with their range represented by hazy or boxed images. His own weapons systems are represented as icons showing readiness status and other variables. The status of his aircraft, including flight direction, elapsed time, altitude, ground speed, and whatever else he needs to know, is presented in a simplified format. Such systems are not as far away as might be expected. The first-generation systems will be in use before the end of the 1990s.

Navigation

In the early days of helicopter flight, navigation was a relatively unimportant concern. Most helicopter flights were of short duration and flown at low enough levels that roads could be followed or landmarks easily spotted. As the capabilities of helicopters increased, however,

Top right: Night-vision goggles, which multiply moon, star, and other ambient light to enable the pilot to see clearly at night, have extended the range of night operations.

25

flights of longer duration became commonplace. It is now possible for such large transport helicopters as the CH-53E, with aerial refueling, to fly a distance of nearly 1,900 miles. Accurate navigation is necessary not only to get the helicopters to their destination but also to enable them to meet refueling tankers along the way.

By the mid-1960s and the Vietnam War, helicopters from rear-area bases were routinely making long-distance flights and flying at high altitudes to avoid ground fire. Ground-based navigational aids were either nonexistent or unreliable; landmarks were often obscured by cloud cover, especially during the lengthy monsoon season. Until the Vietnam era, most helicopter flights were made only by day in clear weather. But Vietnam demanded all-weather as well as night flying, and navigational techniques became extremely important.

Equipping helicopters with radar navigational aids solved the problem until the North Vietnamese and Viet Cong became sophisticated enough to detect and track helicopters by their electronic signatures. This quickly eliminated the use of radar navigating schemes except for doppler radars, which project a narrow beam downward ahead and behind the helicopter. From the time it takes the beam to return to the radar receiver, altitude, ground speed, and drift can be measured.

When the final satellite of a new global positioning system called NAVSTAR was launched in May 1989, a new system began to replace all other navigational aids. Seventeen satellites are in orbit and continually broadcast their position. The satellites are so placed that at least three are in view at any one time from any position on Earth. Using the three satellites as reference points, a small, computer-equipped radio receiver on the helicopter calculates the helicopter's position any place on the globe to within a few feet.

Another high-accuracy system under development is based on the standard inertial guidance units (INS) that have all but replaced navigators in fixed wing aircraft. By measuring elapsed time and taking into account aircraft speed and winds affecting the aircraft, the INS, using a sophisticated mechanical gyro system, can locate a destination and guide an aircraft to that destination with a high degree of precision. But this system does not work in helicopters that fly slow and low and spend a good deal of time hovering. A new system developed in Great Britain for the EH101 helicopter replaces the mechanical internal parts of the INS with laser beams that reflect from mirrors carefully placed in a clear ceramic block. Any change in the position of the ceramic block in relation to the laser beams will lengthen or shorten the laser beam's track. A computer tracks the changes, time elapsed, and direction of motion, and then displays the helicopter's position to the pilot in relation to a reference point.

These and other state-of-the-art systems are designed to make it easier for the pilot to fly and fight the helicopter, as well as reduce the need for additional crew members. At the rate that automation of routine tasks is proceeding, it may not be long before only one crew member will be needed to fly and fight a battle helicopter. The other "crew member" may well be a sophisticated computer performing routine tasks and keeping track of the aircraft's status. Certainly, if someone had told the pilots of 20 years ago that they would be able to pinpoint their location anywhere on the planet with the touch of a switch, they would have thought it fanciful science fiction.

Helicopter Weapon Systems

Military tacticians were quick to see the helicopter's potential as a weapons platform. In 1944, German designers mounted an MG34 machine gun on an Fa 223 twin rotor helicopter. The Germans also designed the Flettner FL 282 to carry two depth charges for submarine hunting. Today, most military helicopters are capable of being armed with a wide range of weaponry, whether their mission is troop transport or anti-armor operations. Helicopter-borne weapons break down into the following categories: machine guns, grenade launchers, rockets, missiles, air-to-air weaponry, torpedoes, and mines.

Machine Guns

The single barrel 50 caliber Browning machine gun has been installed on nearly every American military helicopter at one time or another. For instance, the Marine Corps' CH-46 Sea Knight carries the Browning in a door mount, and the gun is operated by the crew chief.

This page: This UH-1D Huey in South Vietnam mounts a .50 caliber machine gun and a battery of powerful searchlights for night operations.

The idea of the helicopter as a gun platform was developed by the United States Army in 1955. A testing facility was set up at Fort Rucker, Alabama, to develop a means of suppressing enemy ground fire during assault operations. By 1962, the new UH-1B Huey had been configured to carry three weapons systems. The first was the XM-6 Quad, which consisted of four M60 7.62mm NATO machine guns, two mounted on either side of the aircraft. They could be aimed and fired remotely by the gunner or fired by the pilot when attacking straight ahead. The second system was the 40mm grenade launcher. The third was the S-11 air-to-ground missile developed in France.

In 1951, General Electric Corporation took a new look at an old weapon, the Gatling Gun. This multibarrel machine gun was designed during the American Civil War. Its several barrels—up to 12—were fixed to a circular ring that revolved when the gunner turned a crank. Ammunition was fed from a hopper or magazine into the breech. The gun was timed to fire a round every time a new barrel rotated into position. The Gatling Gun was very effective both as a machine gun and, with a range of half a mile or more, as a small artillery piece. As early as the 1890s, an electric motor had been used to rotate the barrels, producing rates of fire in excess of 1,000 rounds per minute. General Electric updated the design and renamed it the Minigun. They used an electric motor to turn as many as six barrels at high speeds to produce rates of fire as high as 3,000 rounds per minute. The first miniguns to be used in helicopters were mounted in the AH-1 HueyCobra in 1966, making it the first "gunship."

Since the Vietnam War, a wide variety of machine guns have been used in helicopters of all nations. The French prefer a 20mm Giat M621, which can fire between 350 and 740 rounds per minute. They have also developed the GECAL .50 caliber three or six barrel machine gun, which is replacing the single barrel Browning. Hughes, now McDonnell Douglas Helicopter Company, developed the 25mm M242 Bushmaster. Ammunition is fed into the breech via a linked chain—hence the nickname chain gun—for use on the Bradley M2/M3 Armored Fighting Vehicles. A larger caliber version, the 30mm M230 was designed as the main gun armament for the AH-64A Apache. Soviet designers selected a four barrel .50 caliber machine gun capable of firing 1,200 rounds per minute for mounting on the Mi-24 Hind D. The British use a 20mm rapid firing cannon built by the Swiss firm Oerlikon for use in the British Army Westland Lynx.

Grenade Launchers

The United States Army also experimented with grenade launchers at Fort Rucker. The idea was to saturate a potential landing area with 40mm grenades to kill or chase out enemy troops hoping to interfere with assault landings. Such grenade launching systems proved invaluable in military operations in South Vietnam.

Today, the grenade launching system has become truly sophisticated. The 40mm XM175 grenade launcher built by McDonnell Douglas weighs only 35 pounds and fires 350 rounds a minute. The XM8, a lighter version to be used in light helicopters, also launches 40mm grenades at the same rate. The entire XM8 system, loaded with 150 grenades, weighs only 238 pounds.

Rockets

Unguided, free-flight rockets were first mounted on fixed wing aircraft during World War I for use against observation balloons. These early rockets were barely updated versions of the 18th century Congreve Rocket and used long sticks for stabilization in flight. By the end of World War II, free-flight rockets (FFR) had become quite sophisticated and were in wide use by all Allied air forces.

The use of armed helicopters was pioneered by the French Army during the French-Algerian War (1954–1962). By the time the conflict ended, the French Army had more than 600 helicopters in service, most of them armed. The French military first used the helicopter for troop transport, but the advantage in using them in the assault role as well quickly became apparent. Initial armament consisted of a combination of 36 68mm FFRs and two .30 caliber machine guns, one mounted on each side of the helicopter. The 68mm rockets were later replaced by 72 37mm rockets carried in pods. The United States Army followed French practice, mounting M-3 rocket pods, which carried 24 70mm FFRs apiece, on either side of the UH-1B Huey. The AH-1 HueyCobra carried four improved M-157 or M-159 rocket launchers under the craft's stub wings.

FFRs can be mounted on racks, in pods, or in boxes from which they can be fired either one at a time or in multiples. Most FFRs are solid-fueled and range in size from 70mm up to the 240mm rocket used by the Soviets. Various warheads—such as high-explosive, shaped charges for use against armor, fléchettes for antipersonnel use, illuminates for lighting up battlefields, and even chaff to decoy radar-guided missiles—can be fitted on the rockets.

Missiles

Missiles are steerable by remote means, rockets are not. This is the distinguishing characteristic between missiles and rockets.

As with rockets, the French Army in Algeria was the first to use guided missiles fired from a helicopter. Wire-guided SS-10 and SS-11 missiles were fitted to Alouette IIIs. In the 1973 Arab-Israeli war, the Soviet-designed AT-3 Sagger was fired by infantry troops and from helicopters against Israeli tanks. The AT-3 Sagger took a heavy toll on Israeli tanks and helped establish the feasibility of an anti-armor role for the helicopter. During the Afghan resistance of the 1980s, AT-2 and AT-3 missiles were mounted on Mi-8, Mi-17, and Mi-24 Soviet helicopters for use against ground targets.

All the missiles mentioned above have in common a guidance system known as "Manual Command, Line of Sight" (MCLOS). A missile with MCLOS is steered by commands transmitted to the in-flight missile through a trailing wire attached to the launcher/control system. The wire unreels behind the missile as it travels toward its target. The operator watches the missile through an optical instrument and guides it toward its target. A significant advantage of this guidance system is that the system cannot be jammed. A major disadvantage is that the missile must travel at a slow rate of speed so the trailing wire does not break; this means that the operator is exposed to enemy counterfire for a significant period of time. And if the operator is sitting in a helicopter, he must contend with the aircraft's vibration.

MCLOS missile steering methods have been replaced by computerization. Semiactive Command, Line of Sight (SACLOS) techniques steer the present generation of missiles. The TOW (Tube-launched, Optically tracked, Wire-guided) missile, for example, uses a SACLOS guidance system. The operator centers the target in the sighting system and fires a missile. A flare on the missile's tail is watched by a sensor. A computer measures the angular distance between the center point of the sight (the target) and missile's course. The computer converts these measurements to flight commands and sends the commands along the wire to the missile's flight controls.

Keeping a distant, camouflaged target in sight while in a moving or stationary helicopter is no easy task. The sighting system must be sensitive, yet not so sensitive as to be rendered useless by the helicopter's vibrations. The operator must also have a good field of view. For this reason, most SACLOS sights are mounted on the cockpit roof or even on the rotor mast.

As effective as the TOW missile system is when using SACLOS sighting, the operator is still hampered by sluggish performance since the missile's speed drops with distance. Although SACLOS missiles fly faster than MCLOS missiles, they still travel below Mach 1 speed to preserve the trailing wires and permit the operator to control the missile. Again, these two factors mean a longer flight time, exposing the helicopter to enemy counterfire for a longer period of time.

A third generation of missiles uses the Lock On After Launch (LOAL) sight. The target is illuminated by either a laser or an infrared beam. The source of illumination can be the helicopter launching the missile, another helicopter, or a ground-based operator. An on-board sensor guides the missile to the illuminated target. As long as the target is illuminated while the missile is in flight, the sensors will accurately guide the missile.

The LOAL system has two obvious advantages. First, the missile can be launched on a high trajectory while the helicopter hides behind a hill or a screen of trees or buildings. When the missile's detector spots the patch of illumination marking the target, the missile will fly directly to the

target. Second, the missile can travel at a high rate of speed—Mach 1 or better—reducing exposure time and/or enemy countermeasures.

A fourth form of guidance for missiles is radar. Air-to-sea (AS) missiles are usually radar guided because ships present large targets against an otherwise blank (to radar) background. The usual trajectory of an antiship missile fired from a helicopter carries the missile to several thousand feet of altitude, where the missile's radar can locate the target. The missile then dives toward the sea, losing itself in the clutter thrown up by radar waves bouncing off the sea's surface and thus protecting the missile from enemy counterfire. When the missile reaches an altitude of from three to 50 feet above the surface of the sea, it skims toward its intended target.

During the 1982 Falkland Islands war, both Britain and Argentina used radar-guided missiles. The British Navy's Sea Skua AS missile was almost as effective as the French-built AM.39 Exocets that Argentina used. Two Royal Navy Lynx helicopters were equipped with Sea Skuas, which had not even completed testing yet, and used them to sink at least two Argentinean vessels. The Exocet uses an active radar seeker, which emits a radar signal on a continual basis. While this signal provides a warning to the target ship, the Exocet is still effective since it flies so low that it is often lost in the radar clutter kicked up by the sea.

A fifth guidance system is seen in the fire-and-forget method; once launched, the weapons operator does not need to pay any more attention to it. The Norwegian-designed Penguin is a fire-and-forget missile. The Penguin uses a passive infrared heat seeker to guide the missile to its target; a ship makes a well-defined and quite warm target against the

This page: The TOW-2 antitank missile, which can be launched from several different American and allied helicopters, has a stand-off probe—the long nose—that detonates on contact with the target. The main charge detonates milliseconds later, creating a gas torchlike effect that slices through enemy armor.

cold sea. The Penguin's infrared guidance system has the advantage of leaving no electronic trail either to itself or to the helicopter that launched it. The Penguin (AGM-119) has been adopted by the United States Navy and is deployed on the SH-3 Sea King helicopter.

The hypervelocity missile is a new concept in missiles that could find application in battlefield helicopters. The hypervelocity missile carries no explosive in its warhead. Instead, its power comes from the fact that the faster an object accelerates, the more energy it will have to expend when it strikes a target. The guidance package is contained in the launcher, rather than the solid-fueled missile. At present, the missile is being developed for tank killer potential.

Air-to-Air Weaponry

As helicopters have become more battle capable, it has become more important to counter them. One countermeasure is to equip helicopters with air-to-air missiles and turn them into rotary wing fighters. Surprisingly, fixed wing aircraft are not very good in the antihelicopter role. In numerous real and simulated tests of fixed wing aircraft against helicopters, the experienced helicopter pilot was almost always able to use his low speed and agility to meet the fixed wing aircraft head on. Since the helicopter pilot was firing his weapons from a more stable platform, he had more time to aim and fire than did the fixed wing pilot.

In 1983, extensive testing of helicopter aerial combat "one-on-one" tactics was jointly carried out by the United States Army and Marine Corps at the Patuxent River Naval Air Test Center. An AH-1S SuperCobra was flown against an OH-58 Kiowa. Testing also matched the OH-58 Kiowa against a UH-60 Blackhawk and the AUH-76 prototype. The test results, which matched those run on a variety of computer simulations of helicopter air-to-air battles, showed that, in the words of the project director Duane Simon, "almost every engagement that we flew wound up in a catfight, a climbing, spiralling maneuver just like they did 40 years ago with fixed wing [aircraft]." The rule of thumb, he went on, seems to be the slower in the corners the better, meaning that the helicopter that can make the tightest turn has the advantage.

The question of weaponry for aerial combat is hotly debated. Testing shows that light-caliber miniguns firing 7.62mm cartridges are of limited usefulness against helicopters like the Mi-24 Hind, which has titanium armor. The McDonnell Douglas chain gun concept seems close to ideal for helicopter use. The chain gun permits the rapid fire of heavy rounds, using a chain somewhat like an oversized bicycle chain to move ammunition into the breech. The chain gun can fire heavy ammunition like the M789 round, which can punch through heavy tank armor, at a rate of 625 per minute. The 30mm M230 chain gun cannon is standard equipment on the AH-64A Apache.

The Stinger infrared heat-seeking missile has been extensively tested for helicopter operations. TOW and West German/French HOT SACLOS

guided missiles have also been tested for helicopter air-to-air combat. The West German MBB Bo 105 and MBB/Kawasaki BK 117 light helicopters are both equipped to carry either missile. The United States AH-1 HueyCobra and SeaCobra carry the TOW missile in their "modernized" versions. The United States Marine Corps upgraded version, the SuperCobra AH-1W, also carries the AIM-9L Sidewinder air-to-air missile.

In short, any weapon that can take advantage of the helicopter's unique ability to fly low and slow or high and slow and packs sufficient punch to cripple or knock down an enemy fixed wing or rotary wing aircraft can be considered a candidate weapon for the helicopter's growing air-to-air role.

Torpedoes

The second helicopter to be developed for military service, the Flettner FL 282, was used for antisubmarine warfare. Today, one of the most valuable weapons a navy can possess is an effective antisubmarine force, with the helicopter as its keystone. The helicopter's ability to fly low and slow and hover at will makes the helicopter a particularly useful weapon against submarines. Helicopters produce no wake or engine noises that can be detected by a submerged submarine. This makes torpedoes dropped from a helicopter especially effective.

Helicopter-borne torpedoes are usually smaller (by up to 14 feet) versions of those launched by surface ships or submarines. The most typical helicopter-borne torpedo today is the United States Mark 44 or Mark 46 homing torpedo. The Mark 46, the more current and more widely used of the two, has a range of 6.8 miles, averages 40 knots, can dive to 3,000 feet, and tracks its quarry with active radar. Helicopter-borne torpedoes are dropped by parachute to prevent damage when they hit the water. The torpedo releases the parachute and sinks to a predetermined depth. Its engine then starts automatically. Modern torpedo engines are driven by propellants like monomethylhydrazine, have electric engines powered by high-density storage batteries, or, as in the new American Mark 50 torpedo, have a pump-jet engine that sucks water through an inlet and spews it out through a jet nozzle.

Torpedo guidance is almost always by active sonar. Sound waves are sent out by the torpedo. The sound waves are reflected back by the target, and a sensor in the torpedo's nose measures the strength of the signal. A computer determines how long it took the sound signal to bounce back. In some sophisticated torpedo guidance systems, the computer can also, within broad limits, determine the kind of material causing the signal to be reflected, thus eliminating accidental targets such as whales and other large ocean creatures.

Mines

Mines come in two varieties, land and sea. Both have the same objective: to lie undetected until an enemy soldier or vehicle comes within range and then explode, destroying the unsuspecting target.

The most advanced submarine mine that can be dropped from a helicopter is the United States Navy's Captor. It is essentially a Mark 46 Mod 4 torpedo contained in a tube. Dropped by helicopter into an area where an enemy submarine is expected to pass, Captor settles to the bottom. Its passive sonar then listens for the approach of a submarine. When one is detected, Captor switches on its active sonar to obtain a precise fix and launches itself. Since Captor cannot distinguish between friendly and enemy submarines, friendly submarines must be kept away.

While not itself a mine, the United States Model B57, Modification 1, Nuclear Depth Charge can also be dropped from a helicopter. The B57 carries a five- to 10-kiloton yield warhead and can be carried by the SH-3 Sea King.

Land mines can also be laid by helicopters. In 1977, the United States Army first deployed the M56 Helicopter Antitank Mine Delivery System,

which used the M74 Antipersonnel and the M75 Antitank mines. This system is now being replaced by Volcano, a new distribution system that is lighter and more effective while using the same M74/M75 mines.

In the Volcano system, 40 mines are mounted on a rack; up to four racks can be carried, depending on the helicopter being used. A propelling charge dispenses each mine to a distance varying from 69 to 246 feet from the line of flight. The mines have antihandling devices that prevent their removal. They can be preset to self-destruct after a period of time.

An even simpler distribution system has been developed by FFV Ordnance of Eskilstuna, Sweden. The FFV B028 is a hollow charge antitank mine designed to penetrate the softer armor beneath a tank or an armored personnel carrier. It is a lightweight munition that an individual can drop by hand from a low-flying helicopter. The individual only has to set the self-destruct time desired, pull the safety tab, and then drop the mine out the door. The mine activates after a predetermined time, and its antihandling device prevents it from being moved or deactivated.

Helicopter 2000

No discussion of the helicopter would be complete without a look ahead to rotorcraft designs of the 21st century. There are many plans and

This page: This UH-1 Huey is carrying the Army Mk 56 helicopter antitank mine delivery system, which dispenses antipersonnel and antitank mines.

programs on the drawing board today. But aviation experts believe that two major programs—tilt rotor/tilt wing aircraft and the United States Light Helicopter Experimental (LHX) program—are most likely to have a profound effect upon all helicopter design into the next century.

There is little argument that today's helicopter offers great advantages for getting in and out of tight places where fixed wing aircraft cannot maneuver. But there is also little debate that the helicopter is still a comparatively short-range and slow aircraft. The dream of countless designers has been to build a helicopter that could fly faster and farther. Unfortunately, the most limiting factor in trying to expand the flight parameters of the basic helicopter is the dynamics of the helicopter itself.

This limitation appears to be changing; the flying attributes of the helicopter and the fixed wing airplane are being combined. Designers are working on an aircraft that can take off or land like a helicopter and fly like an airplane. The tilt rotor design enables the aircraft to lift off vertically and then tilt the rotors forward, allowing the aircraft to fly like an airplane. Some designs tilt the whole wing rather than just the rotor. While the concept is not new, it is finally nearing the point of becoming a reality. The technology to make this combination helicopter/plane a possibility is becoming available. It appears that a host of nations see the obvious advantages in developing this type of aircraft and are making it a major priority in terms of research and development.

In the United States, the tilt rotor program is called the V-22 Osprey, and it is discussed in detail in the United States profiles. Although the development of the V-22 Osprey is certainly promising, the Osprey is not without competitors throughout the world. Other nations are not idly sitting by with desires to develop their own technological equivalents to the Osprey. Countries currently looking into the development of tilt rotor or even tilt wing technologies include Japan, the European community, and the Soviet Union.

The Japanese are developing a design of their own. One of the most promising versions, the TW-68, uses a tilt wing design; the entire wing will rotate upward and then forward. Instead of rotors, the aircraft uses standard propellers. According to the company that is developing it, the Ishida Corporation of Nagoya, Japan, this greatly simplifies the dynamic engineering of a tilt wing over a tilt rotor. In direct competition with the Osprey, the TW-68 is likely to fly in the early 1990s. It will be available as both a nine-seat corporate aircraft and a 14-seat commuter plane. A variety of overnight parcel delivery services in the United States and around the world have expressed a great deal of interest in this particular aircraft design.

The European Future Advanced Rotorcraft group (EUROFAR) has also developed an aircraft that is similar to the Osprey, using a tilt rotor design. This aircraft is in a three-year study phase that concludes in 1990. With plenty of government research funding to look at possible commercial developments and long-term benefits, a few of the major companies involved at present are Aerospatiale of France, Messerschmitt-Bolkow-Blohm of West Germany, Agusta/Aeritalia of Italy, CASA of Spain, and Westland of Great Britain.

The Soviet Union is also looking at tilt rotor/tilt wing aircraft design. According to what little is known, the Soviets began working on several military versions of the basic aircraft in 1975, and intelligence sources say that they have had prototypes flying since 1985. If this is correct, production of two variants started in 1987. At present both variants are believed to be in limited use.

The military attack variant, called the Mi-30, is believed to have a two-member crew and be armed with a variety of heavy weaponry. Its missions could include ground attack, air assault, anti-helicopter, forward air control, special operations, and even electronic warfare. The Mi-31 is believed to be a variant of the same basic airframe as is used for the Mi-30. But instead of being an attack aircraft, it is thought to be configured as a troop transport capable of carrying up to 15 combat soldiers.

A third tilt wing aircraft, believed to be in the developmental stages only, is called the Mi-32. This aircraft is likely to be larger than the United States Osprey design. The Mi-32 will probably be an air assault and troop transport aircraft that will carry up to 30 soldiers. This would put it in the same weight and lift class as the Soviet's current Mi-17 transport helicopter. Tipping the scales at more than 18 tons, the heavy plane will have an estimated flight endurance of three to six hours and a top speed of nearly 350 miles per hour. Additional missions for the aircraft could include special operations and electronic warfare.

Soviet helicopter designer Marat Tischenko is the general designer for the Mil Helicopter Company in Moscow. He says that the Soviet tilt wing program has not been without problems. Today, the Soviets still face challenges in a variety of technologies, including the aircraft's cargo-carrying abilities, engine efficiency, and basic airframe design. Tischenko says that while the Soviets are slowing the development of military versions, they are looking at working with other nations to market commercial applications of their tilt wing designs.

The United States Army is looking at developing an entirely new generation of helicopters for the 21st century. These helicopters will be lighter, stronger, faster, and more capable than the most modern helicopters of today. The Army plans to spend upward of $40 billion to purchase nearly 2,500 of these "super-choppers" in a program called Light Helicopter Experimental (LHX). In terms of rotorcraft, this represents the largest purchase of aircraft in the entire history of the helicopter.

According to the Army, the LHX will be a "smart machine," one that will have a great deal of artificial intelligence built in. Not only can the LHX take orders from the two-member flight crew but it can also act like a third crew member, helping plan the mission, select the weapons, route the attack, press the assault, defend the aircraft against enemy fire, and

enable the crew and helicopter to race back across enemy lines to safety. Should the aircraft be hit and damaged while in battle, the helicopter itself can suggest a course of action to take. The aircraft can also actually self-repair the battle damage temporarily so the mission can continue or the helicopter return to base. Once on the ground, it will tell the repair crew, via electronic link up, what has to be fixed or replaced. The helicopter would then self-diagnose the effectiveness of the repairs, run through the systems, and return itself to "flight ready" status.

The 7,500-pound LHX is currently being designed by two teams of defense contractors. The Boeing Helicopter Company has combined with the Sikorsky Helicopter Company to form the "First Team." The "Super Team" is made up of McDonnell Douglas Helicopters and Bell Helicopter Textron. The First Team proposes an aircraft of a more conventional-appearing design, having a main rotor and a rear "tail-in-fin" rotor design. The Super Team, taking a more radical approach to the flight parameters of the helicopter, is introducing a no tail rotor system.

This page: The Light Helicopter Experimental program will require two basic configurations. The first is a utility/transport helicopter, and the second is a scout/attack helicopter.

The Super Team LHX proposal will use a series of louvered jets that will provide the pilot with everything from torque compensation to complete flying control. The idea is that NOTAR is a much safer design. If the helicopter is backed into trees, brush, or power lines, there is no danger of the tail becoming entangled. According to the statistics, up to 20 percent of all helicopter accidents and crashes are due to the tail rotor blades coming in contact with "something." With louvered jets and no tail rotor, the aircraft could theoretically get "down in the dirt" and not have to worry about obstructions damaging the blades in the tail section.

Both aircraft proposals make liberal use of composite materials. Many aircraft analysts believe the days of the metal helicopter and airplane are numbered. These new composites are up to two-thirds lighter than the metals they replace. The composites also reduce the aircraft's radar signature. Although the Army hesitates to use the word "stealth," military experts say the new aircraft designs are going to be much more difficult to detect on radar than their contemporaries. In addition to these composite materials, new engine-exhaust masking systems and avionic "black boxes" enhance the aircraft's stealth characteristics. Composites are appreciably stronger than metals in terms of their tensile strength. They are also much better than metals at providing battlefield protection to crew and vital components in the event of gun or missile damage. Some ballistic experts say that up to 75 percent of the weight currently being built into crew protection—areas hardened with armor—can be eliminated by using composites instead of metal.

Another area of major emphasis in the LHX program will be the electronic avionics and computers that will make this aircraft fly. Much of the information concerning the LHX's avionics remains classified, but it is known that the LHX will be a thinking machine. Computers won't simply report information, they will interact with the crew in virtually all phases of flying. In the helicopter of the future, it is possible that the pilot will be able to actually talk to the aircraft and get information about on-board systems, status of the mission, and more.

The LHX will be not only a ground-attack fighter but also an aerial dogfighter. The aircraft will be capable of mixing it up and winning against everything from other helicopters to much faster long-range fixed wing fighter planes. Army Major General Ronald K. Andreson, Program Manager of the Light Helicopter Family with the U.S. Army Aviation Systems Command, says that the helicopter of the future, when it goes into battle, must be capable of dealing with all threats at ground level as well as from above.

To do that successfully, the Army is developing a new helicopter that will serve in the roles of ground attack helicopter and armed reconnaissance and will also be the rotorcraft equivalent of a Top Gun fighter. The development of new long- and short-range weaponry that will be "brilliant" rather than just "smart" will make this possible. Missiles and rockets for air and ground targets will be used simply by firing them and letting the ordnance find and destroy either a target of opportunity, a pre-designated target, or an incoming threat.

The attack helicopter of tomorrow may also come equipped with a blinding laser system. This system will be capable of temporarily blinding soldiers on the ground, thus eliminating the danger of enemy ground fire. It will also be able to blind the crew of an attacking aircraft, forcing the enemy to break off the attack and lose control of the aircraft. In addition, the laser system would be capable of knocking out the fire control systems of tanks, armored personnel carriers, and a host of other military systems.

Since the helicopter of the future will be much more of an active air and ground fighter than it is today, future designs will sport much more capable electronic warfare and protection capabilities. At present, many helicopters survive by being small, fast, and capable of quick maneuvering. In the future, helicopters will use everything from decoy flares and chaff to deception electronics to defeat the seeker elements in enemy missiles, rockets, and radars.

Contractors will begin to build and deliver the LHX helicopter to the Army by the mid-1990s. Many aircraft experts say that not since the introduction of the first successful helicopter design has there been so much technology about to go into production in the decade ahead. As with the first successful single rotor VS-300 flight made by Igor I. Sikorsky, it appears the world is about to take another step forward in terms of rotor revolution.

SIKORSKY CH-34 CHOCTAW/SH-34 SEABAT
(Sikorsky Model S-58)

Sikorsky's unrivaled design for the S-58 medium-lift helicopter grew out of an early 1950s United States Army request for a helicopter to replace the R-4/5/6 series. On November 7, 1949, the Model S-55 made its first flight. The S-55 was powered by a Pratt & Whitney Wasp 600 horsepower radial engine mounted in the nose. A drive shaft slanted up to the top-mounted pylon that held the three-bladed main rotor. The cockpit was mounted atop the engine and forward of the main rotor and drive shaft housing. The cockpit was a bit cramped, but the arrangement allowed a roomy cargo compartment that seated up to 10 fully equipped soldiers. The S-55 was adopted by the United States Army and Air Force as the H-19A and H-19C Chickasaw, respectively, and as the HO4S-1 by the United States Navy and the UH-19 by the United States Marines.

But the United States Navy needed a more powerful helicopter for antisubmarine warfare (ASW). Sikorsky designed and built the S-58, a more powerful version of the S-55. The S-58 was equipped with the Wright R-1820-84 Cyclone radial air-cooled engine (1,525 horsepower), which delivered almost

three times the power of its predecessor. The transmission was simplified to reduce maintenance and service requirements. The main rotor and tail rotor were changed to four all-metal blades. The landing gear was altered from the four-wheel type used on the S-55 to a tricycle style with a fixed tail wheel. And the cargo compartment was extended to hold 18 fully equipped soldiers.

Tests showed the clear superiority of the S-58, and the Navy placed its first production orders before the prototype was even flown. Designated the HSS-1, the nomenclature was later changed to the SH-34G Seabat in 1962. The Seabat made its first flight at the end of September 1954 and entered the Navy's inventory in August 1955.

The Army and Air Force quickly followed suit, adopting the S-58 as the CH-34 Choctaw. The Army flew the CH-34A and CH-34C versions; the latter had an autostabilization feature developed for the Navy to enable day and night ASW operations. The Marine Corps purchased the S-58 as the UH-34D Seahorse. For amphibious operations, the Marines also acquired a pontoon-equipped version, which was designated the UH-34E.

The United States Coast Guard also purchased the S-58, designated the HH-34F. The Choctaw/Seabat remained the major medium-lift helicopter in all U.S. military services until replaced in the mid-to-late 1960s by the CH-46 Sea Knight and CH-47 Chinook.

In 1956, the Westland Aircraft Company obtained a license from Sikorsky to build the S-58. Instead of using a radial piston engine as Sikorsky had done, Westland installed a Napier Gazelle gas turboshaft engine, seeking to overcome the one deficiency of the Sikorsky design, lack of power. They also used an automatic flight control system built by Louis Newmark, Ltd. This system, which permits an automatic transition to and from hover and turns onto preselected headings, increased the new helicopter's utility in ASW warfare. Later, two Bristol Siddeley Gnome turboshaft engines were substituted for the Gazelle. This Westland version was called the Wessex and first entered service on July 4, 1961, with No. 815 Squadron. Wessex helicopters have been in service with the British military ever since. The S-58 was also built by Sud Aviation in France for both the French and Belgian military services.

SIKORSKY CH-34 CHOCTAW/ SH-34 SEABAT	
Main rotor diameter:	56 ft.
Tail rotor diameter:	9 ft., 6 in.
Length:	38 ft., 6 in.
Width:	12 ft.
Height:	15 ft., 11 in.
Weight (maximum take-off):	13,000 lbs.
Cruising speed:	122 mph
Maximum altitude:	9,500 ft.
Range:	247 miles
Date of first flight:	1954

Left: An H-34 Choctaw airlifts an M101A1 105mm Howitzer during airlift demonstrations at Ft. Rucker, Alabama. **Right:** A Sikorsky SH-34G Seabat plucks astronaut Alan B. Shepard, Jr., from the sea after his historic suborbital flight in 1961.

BOEING CH-46 SEA KNIGHT
(Vertol Model 107)

The Boeing Sea Knight is a further development of the tandem rotor concept that began in the United States military service with the Piasecki HRP-1 "Flying Banana." In 1956, Vertol Helicopter Company (acquired by Boeing Aircraft Company in 1961 as the Boeing Vertol Company and now known as the Boeing Helicopter Company) began to design an improved medium-lift helicopter, which it designated the Vertol Model 107, for civilian as well as military use. The United States Army ordered 10 of the first prototype, the YHC-1A, for testing but found them too small. The Army then switched its attention

to the larger Model 114, which Vertol had developed from the 107. The Army later adopted this model as the CH-47 Chinook.

But the United States Marine Corps and United States Navy found the Model 107— equipped with a slightly more powerful set of General Electric GE-8B engines—acceptable as a medium assault and transport helicopter. The Marines and Navy adopted the Sea Knight as the HRB-1 in February 1961. The following year, in a reordering of all United States military aircraft designations, the Sea Knight was given the Marine designation CH-46. The Navy designation for the

Sea Knight is HH-46 when equipped for search and rescue and RH-46 when set up for mine countermeasures or mine clearing. The CH-46 Sea Knight reached Marine Corps squadrons in early 1965 and were promptly sent to active duty in South Vietnam.

The Sea Knight is a twin rotor, twin engine medium-lift helicopter. The two three-bladed rotors turn in opposite directions to eliminate torque; therefore, the helicopter does not need a tail rotor. The twin General Electric T58-16 turboshaft engines deliver 1,870 horsepower each in the current E model but only 1,400 horsepower in the earlier D and F

Left: A U.S. Marine Corps CH-46E medium transport helicopter in flight. **Right:** Marine Corps CH-46E helicopters in NATO camouflage return to their base at Yuma Marine Corps Air Station, Arizona.

models. The earliest A model engines delivered only 1,250 horsepower each. The engines are mounted on either side of the aft pylon. The forward rotor, which is mounted on the front pylon, is linked to the engines by a high-speed drive shaft running through a tunnel atop the stressed-skin fuselage. Either engine can drive either rotor, and one engine can drive both.

The large (by helicopter standards) cockpit seats the pilot and copilot side by side. The cargo hold, 24 feet long, six feet wide, and six feet high, is the crew chief's station. The cargo hold is equipped with a large side door and a rear ramp and can carry 25 fully equipped troops. Light vehicles can be driven into the cargo hold. Standard tie-down systems and cargo nets are used to secure cargo. Fold down canvas seats serve troops and passengers. When used as a medevac helicopter, as many as 15 stretchers can be accommodated. The Sea Knight's fuselage is sealed so that it can, in theory, land in calm seas. But even though helicopters can be made watertight, the array of main and tail rotors as well as high-mounted engines makes them unstable on the water unless the rotors are turning.

While the CH-46 is normally unarmed, for protection while in combat zones it can be equipped with either a 7.62 millimeter NATO or a .50 caliber door-mounted machine gun manned by the crew chief. The United States Navy's RH-46 Sea Knight can be fitted with the Mark 44 or Mark 46 antisubmarine torpedoes. The Swedish Navy uses the CH-46 in the antisubmarine warfare role as well; designated the HKP4, they are armed with the FFV Tp 427 antisubmarine torpedo.

The United States Navy and Marine Corps purchased 624 Sea Knights before production ended in the early 1970s. Since then, the Sea Knight has been produced under license by Kawasaki of Japan as the Model KV-107/II. As the Sea Knights began to age, a series of upgrade programs was instituted that will al-

Left: The crew of a U.S. Navy CH-46 Sea Knight stationed at the Norfolk, Virginia, Naval Air Station practice sea recovery operations. **Right:** A Navy CH-46E Sea Knight takes off from the deck of an Iowa-class battleship.

low the Sea Knight to continue to fly well into the next century. All earlier D and F models are slated to be up-rated to the more powerful E model. Glass fiber blades were manufactured and retrofitted throughout the 1980s. A long-range Navy/Marine Corps improvement program was begun in 1981. Called the SR&M (Safety, Reliability, and Maintainability), its goal is to reduce operating costs and extend the life of the helicopter. The CH-46 in its numerous variations is flown by the United States Marine Corps and Navy as well as the military services of Canada, Japan, Sweden, and Thailand.

BOEING CH-46E SEA KNIGHT

Rotor diameter:	51 ft. (both)
Length:	44 ft., 7 in.
Width:	12 ft., 8 in.
Height:	16 ft., 9 in.
Weight (maximum take-off):	21,400 lbs.
Cruising speed:	150 mph
Maximum altitude:	10,000 ft.
Range:	222 miles
Date of first flight:	1958

Far left: A Marine Corps CH-46A takes off for a practice mission. **Left:** A CH-46E during Gallant Eagle exercises ferries a load of assault troops into a landing zone. **Right:** In the desert near Yuma, Arizona, Marines practice assault tactics with two CH-46E Sea Knight helicopters.

KAMAN SH-2 SEASPRITE
(Kaman Model K-20)

The Kaman Seasprite has one of the longest records of service of any United States military helicopter, exceeded by only a few months by the UH-1 Huey. Charles H. Kaman, a former Sikorsky employee and one of the foremost American helicopter pioneers, had developed a different flight control system for helicopters that did not angle the blade to change pitch. In his system, hinged trailing-edge flaps, or "servo-tabs" as he called them, on the outer portion of each blade moved to change the blade's angle of attack. Kaman applied this system first to his intermeshing rotor HTK-1 training and HOK-1 observation helicopters for the United States Navy and later to the United States Air Force's H-43 Huskie.

Kaman next turned his attention to winning a mid-1950s Navy competition to design a high-speed, all-weather helicopter. Instead of his trademark eggbeater rotors, he developed a more traditional design that used a single main and tail rotor. But the design also employed his servo-tab blade-control mechanism. The result was the HU-2 Seasprite.

The Seasprite had a retractable landing gear, a watertight hull, and a surprisingly small fuselage that could still carry 11 passengers. The Seasprite was fitted with folding rotor blades and a cable haul and tie down system, first pioneered by the German Navy during World War II. The nose could even open and fold back to reduce the aircraft's length when stowed aboard ships or aircraft carriers. The fuselage was a monocoque configuration with a stressed metal skin. The Seasprite has been in United States Navy service since it was first introduced in December 1962. The SH-2 design has been so successful that three separate production runs have been made: the original, which terminated in the 1960s, a second in 1972, and a third in 1982–86.

The initial production UH-2A (the designation was changed to SH-2A in the 1962 re-

numbering of all military aircraft) was powered by a single 1,250 horsepower General Electric T58-GE-8B turboshaft engine mounted ahead of the main rotor. Initial shipboard service in 1963 on the USS *Independence* and the USS *Albany* showed that the craft was underpowered, and in 1965 Kaman redesigned the helicopter to accept two GE T58 engines in an outboard mounting on either side of the main rotor housing. These engines provided much improved performance plus the safety of an additional engine for operations over water. Starting in 1967, all single engine SH-2A/Bs were converted to the twin engine model SH-2C.

This up-rating began a practice that has almost become a Navy tradition. Few helicopters have been modified and up-rated as

much as the Seasprite to keep the aircraft up-to-date nearly 30 years after it entered service. And the Seasprite will certainly still be flying in its 40th year.

The need to arm naval helicopters conducting search and rescue missions over hostile territory became clear during operations over North Vietnam and Viet Cong-controlled areas of South Vietnam. The HH-2C armed version of the Seasprite carried a 7.62 millimeter NATO minigun in a chain turret, .50 caliber or .30 caliber machine guns mounted in the waist doors, and armor plating at all critical areas. A subsequent HH-2D version was left unarmed and unarmored.

Two HH-2Ds were further modified by installing radar systems under the helicopter's nose to detect surface ships and surfaced sub-

Left: The crew of an SH-2F Seasprite LAMPS I helicopter runs down their checklist before lifting off for a mission in the Mediterranean Sea. **Right**: An SH-2F Seasprite is refueled on the deck of the carrier USS *Franklin D. Roosevelt* in the Mediterranean Sea. A Soviet Kynda-class missile cruiser sails nearby.

marines. This ultimately led to the Light Airborne Multipurpose System (LAMPS) program to convert all SH-2s to SH-2F standards and deploy them for antisubmarine warfare, anti-ship surveillance and targeting, and search and rescue operations.

The main rotor of the SH-2F is the Kaman four-bladed 101 System. The hub is made of titanium, and the blades, which can be folded, are of aluminum and glass fiber. The tricycle landing gear has two wheels per side in front that fold forward. The fixed rear landing gear has a single tire and is steerable. Two General Electric 1,350 horsepower T58-GE-8F turboshaft engines provide the power. The SH-2F can carry 476 U.S. gallons of fuel. It can also be fitted with two external tanks and can be refueled ship-to-helicopter, while the aircraft is hovering.

The SH-2F carries a crew of three: pilot, co-pilot/tactical coordinator (also known as a Taco), and sensor operator. When fitted for the LAMPS role, the electronics of the SH-2F include surveillance radar; tactical navigation systems; UHF radios; magnetic anomaly detector; sonobuoy receiver, recorder, and data link; sonobuoys; eight Mark 25 smoke markers; up to two Mark 46 torpedoes; cargo hook; and rescue hoist.

KAMAN SH-2F SEASPRITE	
Main rotor diameter:	44 ft.
Tail rotor diameter:	8 ft.
Length:	40 ft., 6 in.
Width:	12 ft., 3 in.
Height:	13 ft., 7 in.
Weight (maximum take-off):	13,500 lbs.
Cruising speed:	150 mph
Maximum altitude:	22,500 ft.
Range:	431 miles
Date of first flight:	1959

Left: A Seasprite in the U.S. Navy's HSL-30 squadron picks up a downed pilot during search and rescue training. Right: An SH-2F Seasprite LAMPS I helicopter during an antisubmarine warfare mission. Visible under the starboard landing gear (the yellow, perforated metal cone) is an ASQ-Magnetic Anomaly Detector.

SIKORSKY SH-3 SEA KING
(Sikorsky Model S-61)

While the Sikorsky Model S-58 proved to be quite a bit more powerful and versatile than its predecessor, the S-55, it still could not carry a sufficient payload to enable it to operate alone in the antisubmarine warfare (ASW) mode. In 1957, the United States Navy issued a request for proposal for a new ASW-capable helicopter that could carry out both the hunter and killer roles. Previously, two SH-34 Seabats had been used as a team, one serving as the hunter, the other as the killer.

The new helicopter, designated Model S-61, was a further improvement on the S-58 (which traced its lineage to the original Sikorsky R-4). The S-61 was developed as an amphibious, all-weather craft that could also serve in the transport and search and rescue roles. Powered by two General Electric T58-GE-8 engines, the new helicopter could carry a full complement of ASW electronics, including a Bendiz AQS-13B, AQS-13F, or AQS-18 dipping sonar; doppler radar and radar al-

timeter; active and passive sonobuoys; smoke markers and smoke floats; and Texas Instruments' AQS-81(V) Magnetic Anomaly Detector. The S-61 can also carry 840 pounds of weapons, including the Mark 44 or Mark 46 homing torpedo. Weapons capacity has been up-rated in later versions to close to 8,000 pounds. In September 1961, the first deliveries of the Sikorsky S-61, Navy designation SH-3 Sea King after 1962, were made to the Navy's VHS-3 Squadron at Norfolk,

Left: Two U.S. Navy SH-3 Sea Kings on an antisubmarine warfare mission. The Sea King was the first Navy helicopter large enough to combine the roles of submarine hunter and submarine killer. **Right:** This Navy SH-3F has lowered its Bendix AQS-13B dipping sonar below the surface to listen for a hostile submarine.

Virginia, and VHS-10 Squadron at San Diego, California. The SH-3 Sea King thus became the first practical ASW helicopter in service anywhere in the world.

The SH-3 is capable of landing on water and remaining stable even in fairly heavy seas as long as the rotors are turning. Two pontoon like floats carried in pods that extend from either side of the fuselage provide additional support to the amphibious hull.

The SH-3 has both a fully functional autopilot and autostabilization system, which are linked to doppler radar and radar altimeter. This allows the pilot to program a set course for the helicopter to fly while hunting a submarine.

The Sea King in its current models was given up-rated T58-GE-8R turboshaft engines that deliver 1,500 horsepower each. This uprating improves performance when carrying

a full weapons load, which can include the MB57 Mark 1 Nuclear Depth Charge. The engines are mounted above the cockpit and drive the five-bladed rotors. Since the SH-3 was designed primarily for shipboard use, the rotor blades fold automatically. The tail rotor also folds for storage.

The S-61 has found a variety of uses that its designers probably did not foresee. The United States Air Force liked the large cargo

Left: A Navy Sea King is guarded by its crew chief during a search and rescue mission. Note the rescue hoist mounted above the open door behind the cockpit. Right: An SH-3F Sea King antisubmarine warfare helicopter takes off from the Belknap-class guided-missile cruiser USS *Biddle*. Note the Sea King's hangar just forward of its nose.

compartment as well as the powerful 1,500 horsepower engines. The Air Force acquired the S-61 for search and rescue operations at a time when long-range penetration of North Vietnam to rescue downed American fliers had become a growing concern. The Navy has used the S-61 as a minesweeper (RH-3A) and has armed it with a 7.62 millimeter NATO minigun, extra fuel capacity, armor, and a high-speed rescue hoist for its search and rescue mode (HH-3A). The S-61 also forms part of the fleet of helicopters belonging to the Executive Flight Detachment in Washington, D.C., which is responsible for transporting the President as well as other senior administration executives.

The Canadian Air Force purchased 41 Sikorsky S-61s, which they designated the CH-124. Sikorsky has also built the S-61 for the navies of Brazil and Spain. The S-61 is also built by Agusta of Italy, Mitsubishi of Japan, and Westland of Great Britain. Agusta-built S-61s have been sold to the Italian Navy and Air Force and the Iranian Air Force. Mitsubishi-built S-61s have equipped the Japanese Marine Self Defense Force. Westland builds derivatives of the S-61 for the British military as the Sea King (Navy) and Commando (Army).

SIKORSKY SH-3D SEA KING

Main rotor diameter:	62 ft.
Tail rotor diameter:	10 ft., 7 in.
Length:	54 ft., 9 in.
Width:	16 ft., 4 in.
Height:	16 ft., 10 in.
Weight (maximum take-off):	18,626 lbs.
Cruising speed:	166 mph
Maximum altitude:	4,900 ft.
Range:	625 miles
Date of first flight:	1959

Left: A Navy technician makes final adjustments to the towed body of a Magnetic Anomaly Detector (MAD) before an antisubmarine warfare mission. **Right:** An SH-3 Sea King towing the MAD detector. MAD detects the presence of a submarine by measuring the disruption in the Earth's magnetic field caused by a submarine's metal structure.

BELL UH-1 IROQUOIS (HUEY)
(Bell Model 204)

There is perhaps no more successful helicopter ever designed and built for military or civilian use than the UH-1 Iroquois, better known as the Huey after its original U.S. military designation, HU-1. The Huey has been up-rated far beyond its original capabilities and remains the most widely used utility helicopter in the United States armed forces.

The UH-1 Huey, the mainstay of American and Army of the Republic of Vietnam forces during the Vietnam War, first flew as Bell Helicopter's Model 204. The Model 204 was originally designed as a light utility helicopter to meet the specifications of the United States Army's XH-40 program. The Huey entered military service as the HU-1A and went to Vietnam as an air ambulance in 1962.

The Huey was the first production helicopter to be equipped with a gas turbine engine. The original engine was a Lycoming T33 capable of developing 770 horsepower. The overall weight of the Huey in its A configuration was 5,800 pounds. As Lycoming engineers improved the T33 engine's performance until it was capable of developing 1,100 horsepower, Bell engineers were able

Left: Assault troops get ready to rappel from a UH-1D Huey.
Right: The UH-1H Iroquois (Huey) entered service in 1959 and remained in use by the U.S. Army longer than any other helicopter.

to build an even larger airframe, the UH-1H. The UH-1H could carry up to 14 fully equipped troops or six stretcher casualties compared with the eight soldiers or three stretchers of the earlier UH-1.

The UH-1H (Bell civilian designation: Model 205) is powered by a T53-L-13 gas turbine engine. The Huey was the first U.S. military helicopter to have an engine mounted on top of and behind the cabin roof. This type of mounting eased the problems of gearing the main shaft and tail rotor and left the cargo and cockpit space clear of drive shafts and engine bulkheads. Five separate fuel tanks hold a total of 223 gallons of fuel.

The fuselage is of monocoque construction, covered in sheet metal. In monocoque construction, the skin covering the fuselage absorbs most of the stress, allowing use of a relatively light tube-steel framework. The pilot sits in the left-hand seat, the copilot or weapons operator in the right. When configured as a troop carrier or gunship, the crew chief serves as door gunner. When configured as an ambulance, a medic is often carried in the main compartment.

The rotor system derives from the successful system developed by Bell and first used on the Bell H-13 (Model 47). The rotor blades themselves originally were extruded aluminum spars laminated together. These blades are now being replaced by stronger blades of glass fiber composite over a NOMEX honeycomb core construction. The trailing blade edge is also glass fiber. The leading edge has a polyurethane covering over a stainless steel sheath, which enables the blade to cut through unexpected obstructions like small tree branches when the aircraft is flying at low altitudes.

The UH-1H carries standard avionics equipment including UHF, FM, and VHF radios; an identification, friend or foe system; and various navigation aids. Bell also offers an optional cargo hook, rescue hoist, and additional fuel tanks.

Left: U.S. Army Reserve UH-1H Hueys fly a practice mission in Honduras; National Guard and Reserve troops are engaged in road-building exercises there. **Right:** U.S. Army UH-1H Hueys serve in a wide variety of roles wherever U.S. military personnel are stationed around the world.

Since more than 7,000 UH-1s of various configurations have been purchased by more than a dozen nations, the Bell UH-1 has been armed with just about every type of weaponry that a helicopter of its weight and payload capacity can carry. Unless operating in a war zone, most Hueys on military service are unarmed. But if there can be said to be any standard armament for the Huey, it is probably three 7.62 NATO M60 machine guns, one mounted on each skid and one in a door mount operated by the crew chief. In addition, the Huey can carry various-sized containers of 2.75-inch free-flight rockets. The Huey may carry other weapons systems, including but not limited to 20 millimeter and 25mm cannons in pod mounts, 7.62mm NATO miniguns, .50 caliber machine guns, rocket launchers up to 3.2 inches, 40mm grenade launchers, various antitank missiles, various air-to-ground missiles, and for naval service, depth charges and Mark 44 and Mark 46 torpedoes.

A twin-engined version of the Huey, the UH-1N Iroquois, is powered by the Pratt & Whitney Canada T400-CP-400 Turbo "Twin Pac," which consists of two PT6 turboshaft engines coupled to a single transmission. The UH-1N, which is flown by the United States Air Force, can be armed with two seven-tube launchers for 2.75-inch free-flight rockets and either two General Electric 7.62mm NATO miniguns or two 40mm grenade launchers.

The United States Army modified numerous UH-1Hs to the EH-1H configuration to provide a tactical battlefield electronic countermeasures capability for a project called Quick Fix I. The EH-1Hs were provided with a radar warning receiver, airborne communications interception equipment, chaff and flare dispensers, and an infrared jammer. The Army also converted 220 UH-1Hs to UH-1V medevac helicopters.

The famed Huey has been flying for U.S. military services since 1962 and will contin-ue to do so well into the 21st century. They will continue to perform resupply, troop carrying, electronic warfare, medical evacuation, and mine dispersing operations as needed. Today's Huey is far more capable than the first UH-1As and UH-1Bs that saved so many lives in Vietnam. The Hueys of tomorrow will be even more capable after they are fitted with new composite blades, radar altimeters, infrared jammers and suppressors, new chaff and flare dispensers, and improved avionics and communications equipment.

The Bell 204/205 model in civilian and military configurations has been built by Bell, by Agusta in Italy, and in Japan and Taiwan under license. No other aircraft has been built for military service in any country in such quantity since the end of World War II than the venerable Huey.

BELL UH-1H IROQUOIS (HUEY)

Main rotor diameter:	48 ft.
Tail rotor diameter:	8 ft., 6 in.
Length:	57 ft., 9.5 in.
Width:	9 ft., 6.5 in.
Height:	11 ft., 9.75 in.
Weight (maximum take-off):	9,500 lbs.
Cruising speed:	127 mph
Maximum altitude:	12,600 ft.
Range:	318 miles
Date of first flight:	1961

Left: Hueys are small enough that up to seven can be packed inside the spacious interior of the U.S. Army's C-5B cargo plane. **Right:** The Bell UH-1 Iroquois serves in the military organizations of more than 25 nations, including the West German Army shown here.

Left: The versatile Huey airlifts a Gamma Goat vehicle in South Vietnam. Right: The UH-1 Huey, classified as a utility helicopter by the Army, can perform almost any assigned task. Medical evacuation is perhaps its most appreciated role.

BOEING CH-47 CHINOOK
(Vertol Model 114)

The United States Army, looking to the central European battlefield in the mid-1950s, developed specifications for a helicopter able to operate in all weather conditions and carry the Pershing medium-range guided missile. The Army design specifications also required that the new medium transport helicopter be able to carry a payload of 4,000 pounds internally and 16,000 pounds externally when suspended from a sling arrangement beneath the air-

craft. They also required accommodation for 40 fully equipped troops as well as a cargo ramp and rear clamshell doors that could be opened wide enough to permit light vehicles to drive on and off.

The Vertol Company, one of five companies submitting designs, presented a stretched and up-engined version of their Sea Knight design. Vertol's design won the competition, and the first order for test helicopters was placed in mid-1959. In the Army's

testing program, the Sea Knight was designated Model YHC-1A and this larger helicopter, later called the Chinook, Model YH-1B. Company designations were Model 107 and Model 114, respectively. In 1962, in line with a complete renumbering of all American military aircraft, the YH-1B was redesignated the YCH-47. By 1963, the first Chinooks were deployed for active duty with the 1st Cavalry (Airmobile) Division. In September 1965, the 1st Calvary was ordered to

Left: A CH-47 Chinook crew assists a headquarters staff somewhere in South Vietnam as they move their command post. Right: The CH-47D Chinook evolved from the smaller CH-46 Sea Knight built for the U.S. Marine Corps and Navy.

Vietnam with its complement of CH-47A Chinooks.

There have been four models of the Chinook developed since 1963. The first, the A model, was powered by two 2,650 horsepower Lycoming T55-L-7 turboshaft engines, a modification of the engines used in the prototypes. The later B model was equipped with two 2,850 horsepower T55-LC turboshaft engines and had improved rotor blades. Model C uses two 3,750 horsepower T55-L11C turboshaft engines, and the D model is powered by two T55-L-712 turboshaft engines, each putting out 4,500 horsepower.

The CH-47 Chinook is similar in appearance and design to the CH-46 Sea Knight. But the two can be differentiated, even when the length of the fuselage is not readily apparent, by the podlike fairings along both sides of the CH-47 in place of the stub wings on the CH-46. The landing gear also serves to differentiate the two helicopters. The CH-47 has two sets of two wheels forward and two single wheels aft, while the CH-46 has a tricycle landing gear.

Like the CH-46, the CH-47's twin main rotors turn opposite to one another and are mounted on twin fore and aft pylons. Each main rotor has three blades that can be folded alongside one another for transportation by fixed wing aircraft or surface ships. The blades used in the D model are of glass fiber and NOMEX honeycomb construction. The two engines are mounted in pods on either side of the rear pylon and drive both rotors. Either engine can power both rotors.

The fuselage is a monocoque construction, covered with sheet metal and glass fiber panels. The bottom half of the fuselage is sealed for "on-the-water" activities. The rounded pods that run three-quarters of the length of the fuselage on either side are divided into sealed compartments to add additional buoyancy. The rear cargo ramp can be completely lowered while the helicopter is on the ground, in flight, or on the water. For wa-

Left: During Gallant Eagle exercises, a CH-47 Chinook hauls cargo in nets slung below the fuselage. The Chinook can carry up to 16,000 pounds of cargo in this manner. Right: A CH-47 Chinook, with its tail ramp open, unloads Navy SEALS during a special operations warfare mission.

ter surface operations, a plastic dam is inflated when the cargo ramp is opened. The cabin, or cargo, area is 30 feet 2 inches long, 7 feet 6 inches wide, and 6 feet 6 inches high, and comes equipped with reversible floor strips that are smooth on one side and have rollers on the other for loading cargo. Up to 44 fully equipped soldiers or 24 stretchers can be carried inside. Hooks slung beneath the aircraft enable it to carry cargoes from water tanks to D5 bulldozers (24,750 pounds) to such artillery pieces as the M198 155 millimeter howitzer (15,600 pounds).

The normal CH-47 crew consists of a pilot, a copilot, and a crew chief. The crew chief occupies the jump seat directly behind the pilot and copilot. If passengers or cargo are carried, one or more load masters are included. Passengers, troops, or paratroops are accommodated in red nylon sling seats that fold up against the cabin wall when not being used.

The approximately 493 CH-47A/B models that remain in United States Army service will be converted to the D model configuration by 1993. In this rebuild program, four aircraft per month are stripped down to the airframe and completely rebuilt. Everything is replaced except the basic airframe, landing gear, and seats. When the earlier models are rebuilt to the up-rated D configuration, they have more than double their original payload capacity.

BOEING CH-47D CHINOOK

Rotor diameter:	60 ft. (both)
Length:	51 ft.
Width:	12 ft., 5 in.
Height:	18 ft., 7.8 in.
Weight (maximum take-off):	50,000 lbs.
Cruising speed:	181 mph
Maximum altitude:	15,000 ft.
Range:	115 miles
Date of first flight:	1961

Left: The spacious interior of the CH-47 Chinook is more than apparent here. **Right:** The CH-47 Chinook has undergone three major modifications to increase power and reduce weight since it first entered service with the U.S. Army in 1961.

Left: The CH-47 Chinook was the mainstay of the Army's heavy-lift capability in South Vietnam. Here, a Chinook resupplies Fire Base Berchtesgaden. Right: The CH-47 Chinook can carry up to 40 fully equipped paratroops.

McDONNELL DOUGLAS 530M DEFENDER
(McDonnell Douglas Model 500M)

The wasp-like Defender resulted from the United States Army's Light Observation Helicopter (LOH) competition in the early 1960s. The roles allotted to the LOH at that time were medical evacuation, close support, photo reconnaissance, light transport, and observation. Of 12 companies entering the competition, only three—Bell, Fairchild Hiller, and Hughes—were selected to develop five prototypes each. Trials were carried out at Fort Rucker, Alabama, in 1963 and were completed on May 26, 1965. The Hughes entry was announced the winner.

Introduced as the OH-6A Cayuse, only 1,434 of the planned 4,000 helicopters were built when production ended in 1970. The OH-6A was fast and agile as well as durable but far more costly to build than expected. The majority of the OH-6As were used in South Vietnam to support American and South Vietnam forces.

Hughes Helicopter—which became a subsidiary of McDonnell Douglas in 1984—continued to build the OH-6A under the designation Model 500 for civilian use as a corporate helicopter. To expand its market, Hughes developed an armed military model for export and sold it under the Model 500M designation. The Model 500M, which used the same Allison T63-A-5A turboshaft engine as the earlier OH-6A, was introduced in 1968. It has been extremely popular with smaller nations and is, or has been, in service in Colombia, Denmark, Mexico, the Philippines, and Spain. It has been built under license by RACA in Argentina, Kawasaki in Japan, and BredaNardi in Italy.

To keep the 500M current, Hughes developed the 500M Defender (500MD), which carried the Hughes B6M-71 TOW, a wire-guided missile. The TOW missile had first seen action in Vietnam in 1972, when two UH-1B Hueys between them smashed 62 targets in one battle.

The original OH-6A was the first production light helicopter to use a gas turbine engine. The Allison T63-A-5A produced 317 horsepower, de-rated to 252 horsepower for takeoff and 215 horsepower for maximum cruising speed. The engine gave the small helicopter such extraordinary performance that it set 23 world records. The 530MD series, an up-rated version of the 500MD series, uses a more powerful 420 horsepower Allison 250-C-20B turboshaft engine.

The OH-6A Cayuse employed a four-bladed main rotor 26 feet 4 inches in diameter and a single, twin-bladed tail rotor mounted at the end of the tail boom. A vertical, down-pointing stabilizer helped offset engine torque. The helicopters in the 500/530 series can be differentiated from the original OH-6A by the five-bladed main rotor and the tail rotor inside a T-shaped stabilizer.

Five basic variations are offered in the 500/530 series. The 500MD Scout Defender is the basic military version and is now in use in Kenya and by the South Korean Air Force. The Scout Defender carries a wide variety of armament, including 2.75-inch rockets, a 7.62mm NATO minigun, and a 40mm grenade launcher or a 7.62mm chain gun. The 500MD/TOW Defender is an antitank version of the Scout Defender and comes armed with four TOW air-to-ground missiles mounted in two pods. The TOW Defender can be easily

Left: Hughes, now McDonnell Douglas, developed the 530MG Defender from their OH-6 Cayuse, which was better known as the Loach in Vietnam. Right: Three OH-6A Loaches returning to base at sunset.

identified by the TOW pods on outriggers at the rear of the cabin and by the turret, which houses the TOW sight, slung under the nose. This version is used by South Korea, Kenya, and Israel. The 500MD/ASW Defender is equipped for antisubmarine work. It carries surface search radar, a towable magnetic anomaly detector, smoke marker launchers, shipboard haul down winch, and two Mark 44 or Mark 46 homing torpedoes. This version has been purchased by the Taiwan Navy. The 530MF Defender is an assault, support, and anti-armor helicopter, but it can also perform scouting, day/night surveillance, utility, and cargo-lift missions.

The 530MG Defender is the latest version to be offered in this well-tested series. It is powered by the Allison 250-C30 turboshaft engine producing 650 horsepower. The 530MG Defender can carry 2.75-inch rockets, TOW missiles, 7.62mm and .50 caliber machine guns, Stingers, and the 7.62mm McDonnell Douglas chain gun. Based on the larger, more powerful civilian MD 530F Lifter, the 530MG integrates much of the technology that will appear in the Army's Light Helicopter Experimental (LHX) program, which is designed to produce a new light, all-purpose helicopter by the mid-1990s.

McDONNELL DOUGLAS 530MG DEFENDER

Main rotor diameter:	27 ft., 4 in.
Tail rotor diameter:	4 ft., 9 in.
Length:	25 ft.
Width:	6 ft., 4.75 in.
Height:	8 ft., 8 in.
Weight (maximum take-off)	3,000 lbs.
Cruising speed:	137 mph
Maximum altitude:	16,000 ft.
Range:	207 miles
Date of first flight:	1963

Left: The Defender can be armed with two TOW II wire-guided missiles. The M-65 sight is visible on the helicopter's nose. Right: The 530MG Defender demonstrates the same maneuverability and versatility that won fame for its predecessor, the OH-6A, in South Vietnam.

Left: The OH-6A Cayuse was designed as a multirole light military helicopter. Its maximum cruising speed was 150 mph.
Right: This MD530 MG Defender is equipped with two twin TOW wire-guided missile launchers and the M65 sight for day/night visibility use.

SIKORSKY CH-3/HH-3 JOLLY GREEN GIANT
(Sikorsky Model S-61R)

In 1962, the United States Air Force was given the mission of providing resupply and crew changes for the "Texas Towers." These towers were artificial islands resembling oil drilling platforms that were located in the North Atlantic and provided early radar warning of enemy attack. At that time, the Air Force lacked a helicopter with sufficient range and cargo capacity to do the job efficiently. So the Air Force borrowed three Sea Kings from the United States Navy. Air Force personnel involved with the project were so pleased with the performance of the Sea King that they arranged to borrow three more. After the redesignation of all U.S. military aircraft that year, these helicopters were known as the CH-3B.

The following year, the Air Force received permission to acquire a cargo-carrying helicopter. They turned to Sikorsky with a list of changes required in the SH-3 naval version. First and foremost, a more powerful set of engines was requested. Sikorsky installed T58-GE-1 turboshaft engines rated at 1,300 horsepower each. The Air Force also wanted a double-wheel tricycle landing gear and a rear door/ramp that opened and closed hydraulically for drive-on/drive-off vehicle loading. The Air Force also requested extensive changes to system components to lower maintenance requirements, enabling the helicopter to operate away from major bases. These changes included pressurized rotor blades that signaled a need for maintenance, self-lubricating hubs on both the main and rear rotors, an auxiliary power unit to supply electrical and hydraulic power while on the ground, and a winch and hoist with a 2,000-pound capacity. The watertight hull was retained.

The first test flight for the new helicopter, Sikorsky designation Model S-61R, took place in June 1963, and the first operational aircraft, CH-3Bs, were delivered in December of that same year. In February 1966, up-rated T58-GE-5 turboshaft engines delivering

1,500 horsepower each were installed in new aircraft. Subsequently, all CH-3Bs were converted to the new engine. Helicopters with the T58-GE-5 engines received the designation CH-3E.

The Air Force Aerospace Rescue and Recovery Service obtained 50 CH-3Es, redesignated the HH-3E, for search and rescue. They were armed with two 7.62 millimeter NATO miniguns. They were also fitted out with armor, a rescue hoist, self-sealing fuel tanks, and a retractable in-flight refueling probe. The HH-3E made history and became known as the Jolly Green Giant during the early 1970s with a series of deep-penetration raids into North Vietnam, Laos, and Cambodia to rescue downed American fliers during the Vietnam War. All HH-3E search and rescue

helicopters are now assigned to Air Force Reserve and Air National Guard units.

SIKORSKY CH-3E/HH-3E JOLLY GREEN GIANT	
Main rotor diameter:	62 ft.
Tail rotor diameter:	10 ft., 4 in.
Length:	57 ft., 3 in.
Width:	15 ft., 9.5 in.
Height:	18 ft., 1 in.
Weight (maximum take-off):	22,050 lbs.
Cruising speed:	162 mph
Maximum altitude:	11,100 ft.
Range:	465 miles
Date of first flight:	1963

Left: This Air Force HH-3E Jolly Green Giant is equipped with an in-flight refueling probe and a rescue hoist for search and rescue missions. **Right:** An HH-3F Pelican, the Coast Guard version of the Sikorsky HH-3.

SIKORSKY CH-53 SEA STALLION/HH-53 SUPER JOLLY GREEN GIANT
(Sikorsky Model S-65)

In the late 1950s, the United States Army found itself in need of a heavy-lift helicopter that could serve as a basic prime mover of goods, equipment, and personnel. Discussions with Sikorsky led to the development of the CH-54 Tarhe (Skycrane), a very large helicopter that looked as if a bite had been taken from its fuselage. The Tarhe was powered by two turboshaft engines driving a huge six-bladed main rotor; it proved itself by doing yeoman duty in South Vietnam. When the United States Marine Corps needed a new assault and transport helicopter, they also turned to Sikorsky. Using the basic design of the Tarhe, the company developed the CH-53

Sea Stallion (Sikorsky designation Model S-65) class of helicopters.

The CH-53 has a watertight hull with a rear-opening ramp to permit loading of bulky cargo. The cargo hold, equipped with reversible skid-roller strips set into the titanium floor, is 30 feet long, 7 feet 6 inches wide, and 6 feet 6 inches high. Light vehicles and artillery pieces up to the size and weight of a 105 millimeter howitzer can be winched into the hold. A total of 37 fully equipped troops, 24 stretchers loaded on special racks, or up to 8,000 pounds of cargo can be carried. With its rotors turning, the CH-53 Sea Stallion can operate directly on the water,

and its rear cargo ramp can be lowered after an inflatable waterproof dam is erected.

In the Tarhe, the central fuselage section was left open to accommodate specially designed cargo and troop containers. For the CH-53, Sikorsky engineers enclosed this area with light sheet metal to form a "boom and pod" fuselage on which the rear stabilizer and tail rotor are mounted. The cockpit seats three crew members: pilot, copilot, and crew chief in the jumpseat behind the pilot and copilot.

Although the CH-53 uses the same basic main rotor and gearing system as the Tarhe, the transmission has been up-rated for the

Left: This Navy RH-53D Sea Stallion carries 450-gallon auxiliary fuel tanks under the sponsons. Note the rescue hoist mounted above the side door behind the cockpit. **Right:** A Marine Corps CH-53D Sea Stallion airlifts a forklift.

CH-53's more powerful engines. The blades are pressurized to warn of cracks. Since the CH-53 was expected to, and does, operate from aircraft carriers and assault landing ships, the main rotor blades and the tail end of the boom, which carries the vertical/horizontal stabilizer and tail rotor, fold hydraulically.

Normally, the CH-53 is not armed, but it can be configured to carry a fairly wide variety of weaponry. In a combat zone, the minimum armament would be a door-mounted .50 caliber machine gun or a 7.62mm NATO minigun or machine gun.

The CH-53A entered service with the Marine Corps in September 1966 and was sent to Vietnam in January of the following year. The new heavy-lift helicopters moved troops and equipment around the country and hauled combat-ready soldiers into hot landing zones until U.S. forces ceased military operations there in 1973. In the years since, CH-53s have formed the backbone of the Marine Corps' heavy-lift capability.

The CH-53 has been extensively up-rated since the introduction of the initial A model, which was powered by two 2,850 horsepower General Electric T64-6 turboshaft engines. In 1966, the United States Air Force ordered a more powerful version of the CH-53A, powered by twin 3,080 horsepower T64-GE-3 turboshaft engines, to supplement its HH-3 Jolly Green Giants. Designated the HH-53B, they flew long-range search and rescue missions during the Vietnam War and came to be called "Super Jolly Green Giants." An uprated version now in use, the HH-53C, employs two T64-GE-7 engines developing 3,925 horsepower each. The HH-53Cs are also equipped with auxiliary fuel tanks, a retractable in-flight refueling probe, a rescue hook, and an external hoist capable of lifting 20,000 pounds.

The current version of the CH-53 used by the Marine Corps is the CH-53D, which entered service in March 1969. The CH-53D has

Left: The CH-53D is powerful enough to airlift a 20,000-pound Light Armored Vehicle. **Right:** This flight of CH-53 Sea Stallions is equipped for in-flight refueling. Each helicopter can fly 55 fully equipped Marines anywhere within a 2,000-mile radius in a matter of hours.

a unique cargo handling system that permits one man to load the aircraft. The more powerful T64-GE-413 turboshaft engines deliver 3,925 horsepower each and give the helicopter a maximum speed of 196 miles per hour. The T64-GE-413 engine is also far easier to maintain. The CH-53D can carry 55 fully equipped troops. These aircraft took part in the aborted Iran hostage rescue operation in 1980.

The CH-53 is also operated by the United States Navy as a minesweeping helicopter. Designated the MH-53D, it possesses a variety of mineclearing equipment and electronics. Four MH-53Ds aboard the USS *Shreveport* took part in the 1984 Red Sea operation to clear mines placed by Libya in an attempt to shut down that international waterway.

To upgrade the capability of the Air Force's Special Operations Forces, 33 HH-53s have been converted to the MH-53J PAVE LOW III Enhanced configuration. They have been equipped with terrain-following and terrain-avoidance radars, communications equipment for secure communications, titanium armor, and mountings for either a .50 caliber machine gun or the 7.62mm NATO minigun.

The CH-53/HH-53 series has a long history of service with the U.S. armed forces. It has compiled one of the best safety records of all military aircraft flying today. Austria, West Germany, and Israel also fly the CH-53.

SIKORSKY CH-53D SEA STALLION/ HH-53D SUPER JOLLY GREEN GIANT

Main rotor diameter:	72 ft., 3 in.
Tail rotor diameter:	16 ft.
Length:	67 ft., 2 in.
Width:	15 ft., 5 in.
Height:	24 ft., 11 in.
Weight (maximum take-off):	36,400 lbs.
Cruising speed:	173 mph
Maximum altitude:	6,500 ft.
Range:	257 miles
Date of first flight:	1964

Left: The CH-53D Sea Stallion is the mainstay of the U.S. Marine Corps' heavy-lift capability.
Right: An RH-53D Sea Stallion, bound for the Red Sea, is loaded onto a C-5A transport plane.

82

Left: A pair of CH-53s touch down at sunset. Right: Two Marine Corps CH-53Ds practice low-level flying.

BELL AH-1 HUEYCOBRA
UNITED STATES (Bell Model 209)

To the untrained eye, the shorter and far more slender AH-1 HueyCobra looks nothing like its parent, the fat-bodied, lumbering UH-1 Huey. In 1965, Bell Helicopter began to develop a specific Huey variation to serve as an armed helicopter to escort slow, unarmed or lightly armed transports and medevac choppers. Today, the AH-1W SuperCobra is a "do anything, go anywhere" combat helicopter that can fly escort missions or bust tanks.

The HueyCobra first flew in September 1965; by March 1966, the United States Army had placed its first order. Basically, the new helicopter (Bell Model 209) retained the engine, transmission, and other major parts of the Model 205, but replaced the bulky fuselage with a new, thin-profile fuselage. Stub wings were added to ease the load on the main rotor and serve as attaching points for additional weapons. The narrow fuselage dictated a tandem cockpit seating arrangement; the pilot was placed behind and above the copilot/weapons operator.

A turret was mounted under the nose of the fuselage to carry miniguns, rapid firing cannons, or grenade launchers. These weapons were controlled by the copilot/weapons operator, who could slew them in wide arcs either side to side or up and down. When the copilot/weapons operator released the weapon controls, the turret resumed a locked fore and aft position. The copilot/weapons operator could also fly the helicopter from his station. The pilot was able to fire the nose turret weapons from his position but only when the turret was in the locked position. The pilot was responsible for firing the weapons mounted on the stub wings.

The HueyCobra has gone through a number of modifications since it first entered service. Initially, it was intended only as an interim system until the larger, more capable Lockheed AH-56 Cheyenne development was completed. But when the Cheyenne was canceled in 1972, Bell began to plan seriously for up-rated models.

The initial model designation of the Huey-Cobra was AH-1G. The AH-1G was powered

Left: The AH-1 HueyCobra, shown here in its up-rated AH-1S version, was the world's first helicopter specifically designed as a gunship. **Right:** The AH-1S Huey-Cobra is a heavily armed gunship. Note the M197 three-barrel 20mm cannon beneath its nose.

modernized HueyCobra, the AH-1S, could be developed.

Modernized HueyCobras were delivered in three phases. The first AH-1S, which entered Army service in March 1977, had a flat plate canopy instead of the earlier rounded panels, to reduce sun glint. It was also equipped with new, more extensive electronics and the up-rated Lycoming T53-L-703 1,800 horsepower turboshaft engine. The next phase was an up-gunned AH-1S equipped with a new universal turret able to mount either a 20 millimeter or 30mm gun. This version also had other modifications to improve the handling of weapons. The third phase was termed the "modernized" AH-1S. Besides including the improvements of the first two phases, these HueyCobras carried new composite rotor blades, a new fire control system that included a laser range finder, an improved navigation system, and an infrared jammer. All versions fire the TOW missile.

The most recent enhancement for the HueyCobra is the C-NITE project, which provides the HueyCobra with the ability to kill tanks at night. The C-NITE sight uses the tank thermal imager developed for the M-1 Abrams Main Battle Tank and the TOW 2 system video thermal tracker from the Bradley Armored Fighting Vehicle. This new sight allows the HueyCobra to find and destroy tanks at night or in heavy fog or smoke conditions.

Other versions of the HueyCobra include the United States Marines' AH-1T SeaCobra and AH-1W SuperCobra. The AH-1T, which carries a more powerful Pratt & Whitney Canada T400-WV-402, is an up-rated version of the twin-engine AH-1J. The AH-1W Super-Cobra "Whiskey," originally called the AH-1T+, is powered by twin General Electric T700-GE-401 turboshaft engines producing 3,250 horsepower. All AH-1T SeaCobras in the Marine Corps inventory have now been up-rated to the AH-1W configuration.

In keeping with the Marine Corps' self-definition as a "lean, mean fighting ma-

by a Lycoming T53-L-13 turboshaft engine producing 1,100 horsepower. The United States Army acquired the majority of the AH-1Gs produced, but Israel and the Spanish Navy ordered six and eight respectively. The United States Marine Corps ordered a twin engine version, the AH-1J SeaCobra. Two Pratt & Whitney Canada T400-CP-400 twin turboshaft engines coupled to a single transmission provided 1,100 horsepower for the SeaCobra as well as the insurance of an extra engine for over-the-water emergencies.

Soon, however, the Army wanted an attack helicopter powerful enough to cope with the growing threat of Soviet and Warsaw Pact tanks. The B6M-71 TOW provided the Army with a guided missile potent enough to destroy any Soviet main battle tank. The wire guidance system gave the missile the required precision when fired from the relatively long range needed by a hovering helicopter. The first HueyCobra model to be fitted with the TOW was the AH-1Q, which was intended as an interim solution until the

Left: The Marine Corps purchased a twin-engine version of the HueyCobra, called the AH-1W (Whiskey) SeaCobra. Right: An AH-1S HueyCobra during a landing at Fort Campbell, Kentucky. Note the flat plate canopy, which replaced the earlier rounded canopy to reduce sun glint.

chine," the AH-1W can perform missions ranging from anti-armor to search and destroy and target acquisition. The AH-1W can carry a wide variety of armaments: a 20mm three-barrel M197 gun or up to eight Hellfire or TOW missiles and either 76 2.75-inch or 16 5-inch Zuni rockets or, for air-to-air combat, either two 20mm pods or two AIM-9L Sidewinder missiles.

BELL AH-1S HUEYCOBRA

Main rotor diameter:	44 ft.
Tail rotor diameter:	8 ft., 6 in.
Length:	44 ft., 7 in.
Width:	3 ft., 3 in.
Height:	13 ft., 5 in.
Weight (maximum take-off):	10,000 lbs.
Cruising speed:	141 mph
Maximum altitude:	12,200 ft.
Range:	315 miles
Date of first flight:	1965

Far left: The AH-1W SeaCobra's main task is to kill tanks. The sudden appearance of the "Whiskey" would be enough to give any tank commander heart failure. **Left:** This AH-1W SeaCobra is armed with two M20 19-round 2.75-inch free-flight rockets and two quadruple Hellfire missile launchers attached to the stub wings. **Right:** The SeaCobra can provide close air support for Marine Corps amphibious operations. Here, a SeaCobra lifts off the deck of an assault ship and flies past a CH-46 Sea Knight.

Left: This SeaCobra carries Hellfire missile launchers and a three-barrel 20mm cannon. Also note the ALQ-144 radar jammer mounted above the engines and behind the main rotor mast.
Right: A National Guard AH-1S HueyCobra pilot on training deployment in Honduras.

SIKORSKY CH-53E SUPER STALLION/MH-53E SEA DRAGON
(Sikorsky Model S-80)

As useful and powerful as the CH-53 Sea Stallion helicopters were to the United States Marine Corps, there remained a need for an even more powerful heavy-lift helicopter. With the advent of both portable antiaircraft guided missiles and the over-the-horizon concept of amphibious landings, a powerful and fast helicopter was needed to carry massive amounts of supplies and large numbers of fully equipped troops. It was also necessary to then keep those troops resupplied. The Marine Corps and Sikorsky evolved the CH-53E Super Stallion version of the heavy-lift CH-53 Sea Stallion; it flew for the first time in March 1974.

From a distance, the two helicopters appear identical, but a closer look reveals four distinct differences. The first and most obvious difference is the presence of a third General Electric T64-416 turboshaft engine mounted on the transmission fairing above and slightly behind the starboard engine. The extra engine helps the CH-53E reach a top speed of 193 miles per hour, which is fast enough that it can be refueled in flight by a KC-130 Hercules tanker.

The second difference can be found in the extra wide and thick sponsons jutting from either side of the fuselage. These sponsons not only serve to stabilize the huge helicopter when conducting on-the-water operations but also function as fuel tanks that give the CH-53E a total internal capacity of 1,017 gallons. Additional external drop tanks holding 650 gallons of fuel each can be mounted on the sponsons.

The third difference on the CH-53E is found on the tail. The vertical stabilizer and a larger tail rotor are cocked to the right. The horizontal stabilizer forms a gull-like wing and is supported by a strut. The fourth and final difference is found in the blades of the seven-bladed main rotor, which are made of titanium and glass fiber. The earlier CH-53A/D models employ a six-bladed main

Left: The Navy's Airborne Mine Countermeasures MIH-53E Sea Dragon helicopter is flown by HM-12 Squadron of the Atlantic Fleet, based at Norfolk, Virginia. **Right:** The CH-53E Super Stallion can be distinguished from the CH-53D by its seven-bladed main rotor, three engines, and canted vertical stabilizer.

rotor. The blades are attached to the main hub by extension straps that make it appear as if the E model's main rotor is greater in diameter than that of the A/D models.

The extra blade required modifications to the main rotor assembly, particularly the hub, which nearly doubled in size. The main hub is manufactured of steel and titanium and uses elastomeric rather than mechanical bearings. As in the CH-53A/D series, the blades are pressurized to warn of cracks.

The three General Electric T64-416 turboshaft engines are each rated at 4,380 horsepower. The seventh blade, coupled with the new engines, nearly doubles the lifting power of the CH-53E over that of the CH-53A/D, making the Super Stallion one of the most powerful heavy-lift helicopters outside the Soviet Union.

The cargo hold is about the same size as that of the CH-53A/D Sea Stallion, but more cargo can be carried because of the more powerful engines. The CH-53E can carry a maximum payload in excess of 36,000 pounds compared with the 8,000-pound payload of the CH-53A/D. Instead of 37 fully equipped troops, the Super Stallion can carry 55. The CH-53E can also carry up to seven standard cargo pallets. Using its winch and cargo hook, the Super Stallion can carry one LAV-25 (Light Armored Vehicle), which weighs 24,400 pounds, plus add-on fuel tanks.

The cockpit of the CH-53E is similar to that of the CH-53A/D and carries a crew of three. But the instrumentation and flight controls have been up-rated. The Super Stallion uses two computers and a new autopilot in addition to the latest in automated navigation equipment.

The United States Navy flies the MH-53E Sea Dragon for mine countermeasures. Several MH-53Es performed mine countermeasure operations in the Persian Gulf in support of the multinational naval task force deployed there in 1987–88 to keep this international waterway open to all sea traffic. The

Navy version can be instantly recognized by the extremely large sponsons that carry additional fuel to enable the MH-53E to operate for long periods of time. The MH-53E is powerful enough to tow mechanical, acoustical, or magnetic hydrofoil sleds to detect various types of submerged mines.

Normally, the CH-53E and the MH-53E are not armed, but a number of studies to arm this aircraft have been carried out. The helicopter could be fitted with a variety of weapons, ranging from depth charges to AIM-9 Sidewinder missiles for air-to-air combat. In an active combat zone, whether serving in

Left: The massive size of the Super Stallion's main rotor hub is clearly apparent here. The addition of a third engine and a seventh blade quadruples the helicopter's lifting capability. **Right:** The RH-53E/CH-53E Super Stallion is flown by a crew of three—pilot on the left, copilot on the right, and flight engineer behind the pilot and copilot.

the assault/transport role or on search and rescue duties, the CH-53E would be expected to carry either a .50 caliber machine gun or the 7.62 millimeter NATO minigun as a bare minimum.

The CH-53E Super Stallion is a powerful helicopter and, according to experienced helicopter pilots who have flown both versions, handles differently than the CH-53A/D. By the end of May 1987, the CH-53E had suffered six fatal crashes, and the aircraft was grounded for several weeks. Separate naval and congressional inquiries revealed no inherent design flaws, and most crashes were ascribed to the crew's miscalculation of the craft's capabilities. A number of modifications were made during this time, but both investigations showed that the changes had nothing to do with the crashes. The CH-53E has been on full-flight status since the summer of 1988, and no fatal or major nonfatal crashes have been reported. The CH-53E Super Stallion will continue to be flown well into the next century.

The CH-53E Super Stallion is used by the Marine Corps and Navy and has been exported to Israel and West Germany for use in their armed forces. Japan has purchased two MH-53Es for minesweeping duties.

SIKORSKY CH-53E SUPER STALLION/MH-53E SEA DRAGON	
Main rotor diameter:	79 ft.
Tail rotor diameter:	20 ft.
Length:	73 ft., 4 in.
Width:	13 ft.
Height:	18 ft., 7 in.
Weight (maximum take-off):	73,500 lbs.
Cruising speed:	173 mph
Maximum altitude:	9,500 ft.
Range:	1,290 miles
Date of first flight:	1974

Left: A Navy MH-53E tows an Mk 105 hydrofoil antimagnetic mine vehicle in the Persian Gulf. Right: The CH-53E/RH-53E/MH-53E Super Stallion is the most capable heavy-lift helicopter in Marine Corps/Navy service. It can lift 36,000 pounds of cargo and fly for 20 hours when fitted with two 1,015-gallon fuel tanks as shown here.

SIKORSKY UH-60A BLACK HAWK/SH-60B SEAHAWK

UNITED STATES (Sikorsky Model S-70)

In the early 1970s, the United States Army identified a need for a more advanced utility helicopter than the UH-1 Huey that would perform a variety of roles into the next century. A proposal for a program called Utility Tactical Transport Aircraft System (UTTAS) was developed, and in 1972, two companies, Sikorsky and Boeing Vertol, were selected to supply prototypes. In late December 1976, the Army selected Sikorsky as the prime con-

tractor; the first deliveries of the new UH-60A Black Hawk were made in 1978.

The Black Hawk is a traditionally designed helicopter with a single main rotor and a boom-mounted tail rotor. The main rotor can survive hits from .50 caliber or 23 millimeter armor-piercing shells. The rotor hub uses elastomeric bearings that do not need lubrication and require far less maintenance than traditional metal bearings. The blade tips are

swept back 20 degrees, and the trailing edges have tabs to improve airflow. The blades are made of hollow titanium spars, NOMEX honeycomb cores, graphite trailing edges, and glass fiber leading edges, and covered with glass fiber and epoxy skins. The leading edges are sheathed in titanium.

Two General Electric T700-700 turboshaft engines provide 1,543 horsepower each and drive a single transmission. The Black Hawk

Left: An SH-60B Seahawk, equipped with an ASQ-81 Magnetic Anomaly Detector, approaches the landing deck at the stern of the Oliver Perry-class frigate USS *Crommelin*. **Right:** The Sikorsky SH-60B Seahawk was designed to fill the Light Airborne Multipurpose (LAMPS) III role for the Navy.

also carries a Solar 90-horsepower auxiliary power unit, a small gas turbine engine, for operations independent of ground support. The fuel system was designed to be crashworthy—that is, in most crashes the fuel is not expected to catch fire or explode. The fuselage is sufficiently armored to withstand hits from .30 caliber weapons, such as the AK-47 assault rifle and its derivatives. The Black Hawk can be armed with one or two side-mounted machine guns, Hellfire guided missiles, 2.75-inch rockets, and the M56 mine-dispersing system. The Black Hawk carries a crew of three, and the pilot's and copilot's seats are armored. The aircraft can also carry a full infantry squad (11 troops), but as many as 14 soldiers can be crammed into the main cabin in what Sikorsky denotes as "high-density seating." Eight of the seats can be replaced with racks for four stretchers. The Black Hawk is equipped with an external cargo hook with an 8,000-pound cargo capacity. Despite its capacity, the Black Hawk is small enough that one can be carried in a C-130 Hercules, two in a C-141 Starlifter, and six in a C-5 Galaxy transport aircraft.

Since its introduction in 1978, the UH-60A Black Hawk has undergone a number of modifications for specialized missions. The Army developed the EH-60A to carry Quick Fix IIB electronic countermeasures equipment for disrupting and monitoring enemy battlefield communications. The EH-60A can be identified by the four dipole antennae that project above and below the boom and the whip antennae attached beneath the fuselage.

The Air Force ordered a version of the UH-60A, known as the HH-60A Night Hawk, to be used as a combat rescue helicopter. The Night Hawk, armed with 7.62mm NATO machine guns, can conduct rescue missions up to 287 miles distant, day or night, without an escort. The Air Force is also purchasing a second version of the UH-60A, known as the MH-60G Pave Hawk, which is an outgrowth

of the interim Credible Hawk rescue helicopter program. The Pave Hawk is a Night Hawk that will be fitted with special instrumentation, including radar, electronic map displays, tactical air navigation systems, and .50 caliber machine guns.

The Marines have purchased nine VH-60A Black Hawks to replace its VH-1N Hueys in the Executive Flight Detachment of Marine Helicopter Squadron 1, the unit that flies the President and other administration officials.

The Navy has also purchased a variation of the S-70, designated the SH-60B Seahawk, for their Light Airborne Multipurpose System (LAMPS) Mark III program. The Navy's version differs from the Army's in having marinized gas turbine engines (specially constructed engines for operation in a humid,

salty environment), chin pods, pylon mounts to hold either two Mark 44 or Mark 46 homing torpedoes or extra fuel tanks, magnetic anomaly equipment, a fourth crew space for the sensor operator, greater fuel capacity, rescue hoist, automatic blade-folding devices for the main and tail rotors, and a haul-down device for landing the helicopter on small ships in rough seas. The Seahawk can also refuel while hovering.

The Navy is deploying the Seahawk on all Oliver Hazard Perry-class frigates, Spruance-class and Aegis destroyers, and Ticonderoga-class cruisers, a total of 106 ships. The Seahawk is replacing the earlier LAMPS Mark I SH-2D Seasprites and will provide greater range, endurance, and time available to track a target than the Seasprites.

Left: The Sikorsky UH-60A Black Hawk entered regular service with the Army in 1978. Right: The UH-60 Black Hawk can carry 11 fully equipped soldiers.

Another Navy version of the Seahawk, the SH-60F, is being deployed as an antisubmarine warfare (ASW) helicopter to patrol the "inner zone" of an aircraft carrier battle group. Instead of LAMPS equipment, the SH-60F carries specialized ASW instrumentation, including dipping sonar and Mark 50 homing torpedoes. The Navy has also ordered a combat search and rescue version, the HH-60H, that can also support Navy SEAL and UDT (Sea Air Land commandoes and Underwater Demolition Team) special forces.

The Seahawk has been so successful that it has carried out 97 percent of all assigned missions since it entered service. Seahawks are flown by the Royal Australian and Spanish navies. The Japanese Marine Self Defense Force has also ordered the Seahawk to replace its aging fleet of SH-3s.

Sikorsky has marketed an export version of the Black Hawk, the S-70A. The first few S-70As went to the Republic of the Phillipines Air Force and the Royal Australian Air Force. The majority of all other Australian Black Hawks will be assembled by Hawker de Havilland in Australia. Westland of Great Britain, continuing its long association with Sikorsky, will assemble the helicopter from kits supplied by Sikorsky.

SIKORSKY UH-60A BLACK HAWK/ SH-60B SEAHAWK

Main rotor diameter:	53 ft., 8 in.
Tail rotor diameter:	11 ft.
Length:	50 ft., 0.75 in.
Width:	7 ft., 9 in.
Height:	16 ft., 10 in.
Weight (maximum take-off):	16,260 lbs.
Cruising speed:	184 mph
Maximum altitude:	19,000 ft.
Range:	373 miles
Date of first flight:	1974

Left: The UH-60 Black Hawk can be refitted with a standard refueling probe and a rescue hoist for search and rescue missions.
Right: The UH-60 Black Hawk can lift 8,000 pounds on its external cargo hook.

Left: These Army UH-60s demonstrate their versatility by carrying both troops and equipment during an air assault exercise. Right: The Air Force's Night Hawk is a special search and rescue version of the UH-60A. All 10 Night Hawks purchased will be upgraded to the MH-60G Pave Hawk configuration.

McDONNELL DOUGLAS AH-64A APACHE

In 1881 in Arizona, the US Sixth Cavalry fought Apaches led by Geronimo, Chato, Nana, and Juh. Exactly 105 years later, the Sixth Cavalry became the first combat-ready unit to field the AH-64A helicopter. The AH-64A was built in Mesa, Arizona, by Hughes Helicopter, Inc., which became McDonnell Douglas Helicopter Company in 1984, and named in honor of the Apache warrior. The AH-64A Apache is the first day/night, all-weather, anti-armor battle helicopter in the U.S. military inventory.

The Apache grew out of the recognition following the Vietnam War that the United States Army needed a helicopter specifically designed for the attack role. After extensive evaluation of several designs, Hughes' YAH-64 prototype was chosen in 1976. The first production Apache was rolled out on September 30, 1983, and the first delivery to the Army was made January 26 of the following year.

To carry out its anti-armor role, the Apache is equipped with the McDonnell Douglas M230 30 millimeter chain gun and up to 16 laser-guided Hellfire antitank missiles, which have a range of more than 3.7 miles and can penetrate the armor of any known main battle tank. The Apache can also provide suppressive fire against concentrations of light armored vehicles and troops. For this task, it uses the chain gun as well as up to 76 2.75-inch folding-fin aerial rockets that can deliver antipersonnel mines or high explosives. Two soldiers can reload or reconfigure the helicopter's weapons systems within ten minutes.

The Apache is also being tested in the air-to-air role and has been approved to fire the Stinger antiaircraft missile. Its M230 30mm chain gun can be used against other helicopters and fixed wing aircraft.

Left: The AH-64A Apache was specifically designed as a gunship capable of destroying main battle tanks. **Right:** An AH-64A Apache fires a double salvo of 2.75-inch rockets from its 19-tube launchers.

The Apache, while carrying a load of eight Hellfire missiles, 320 rounds of 30mm ammunition, and fuel for 1.83 hours, can climb at the rate of 1,450 feet per minute on what is known as the Army Standard Hot Day, defined as 95 degrees at 4,000 feet altitude. The aircraft can also climb at a rate greater than 3,000 feet per minute in the weather conditions expected to be encountered in central and western Europe—faster than most jet airliners. With external tanks fitted for ex-

tended ranges, the Apache is fully capable of flying itself across the Atlantic.

The Apache was designed to be crashworthy. The fixed landing gear can absorb a straight-down impact at 20 feet per second, and the airframe is designed to collapse in on itself, giving the crew a 95 percent probability of walking away from a crash at up to 42 feet per second. The armored crew seats also absorb impact energy. The canopy protects the crew from fatalities in crashes as

well as helping to prevent the cockpit from being crushed in case of a rollover.

The two General Electric T700-701 turboshaft engines provide maximum continuous power of 1,694 horsepower each and drive the rotor system through individual gear boxes and transmissions mounted in the nose. The engines are mounted far apart—6.6 feet—to minimize the chance of enemy fire damaging both engines at one time. A 125-horsepower auxiliary power unit operates the transmission to start the engines or to provide full electrical power, pressurized air, and hydraulics when the engines are shut down.

The exhaust system is divided into two subsystems. The main exhaust nozzle is immediately followed by three secondary nozzles per engine. In these secondary nozzles, engine cooling air and external air, drawn in through auxiliary inlets, are mixed with the exhaust, reducing exhaust temperature from 1,065 to 580 degrees. This reduces the engine's infrared signature below the level detectible by current heat-seeking guided missiles.

The Apache's main rotor has four blades, each built up from a four-cell box. Stainless steel spars and glass fiber tubes provide reinforcement. The heavy-gauge stainless steel leading edge can withstand striking a tree branch up to two inches in diameter. The trailing edge can withstand damage from .50 caliber machine guns or 23mm high-explosive shells. The tail rotor is composed of two flexible twin-bladed hubs that can be canted from the vertical to reduce noise.

The Apache has two stub wings that provide additional lift. The wings can also serve as attaching points for external fuel tanks or external pylons to carry Hellfire or 2.75-inch rockets. The tail surfaces consist of a fixed vertical stabilizer and a horizontal stabilizer—dubbed a stabilator. The stabilator is mounted aft of the vertical stabilizer and moves as one piece.

Left: The Apache has incredible speed and agility: cruising at 187 mph and climbing at 2,500 feet per minute. **Right:** The AH-64A Apache carries a wide variety of weaponry: 2.75-inch rockets (red), laser-guided Hellfire missiles (blue), and a 30mm chain gun in a moveable turret.

Fuel cells are located forward and aft of the ammunition bay. They are self-sealing against .50 caliber rounds and can absorb the impact of rounds up to 23mm. Against 14.5mm armor-piercing rounds, the cells, which are further protected by foam and backing boards, will self-seal to provide a 30-minute fuel supply. Nitrogen gas purging prevents fire in the event of incendiary-round penetration.

Armor made of boron carbide bonded to Kevlar protects the crew and vital systems. Blast shields separate the pilot and co-pilot/weapons operator from each other; thus, both crew members will not be knocked out by a single round. Armored seats and airframe armor can withstand rounds up to .50 caliber of armor-piercing incendiary shot.

The Apache has a wire strike protection system to sever power or other lines during low-level flights or landings. An upgrade program was defined in 1989 and will be implemented to keep the Apache battle worthy in coming years.

The AH-64A Apache will be the Army's main battle tank killer well into the 1990s. The helicopter is being distributed throughout the Army, the National Guard, and Army Reserves.

McDONNELL DOUGLAS AH-64A APACHE	
Main rotor diameter:	48 ft.
Tail rotor diameter:	9 ft., 2 in.
Length:	48 ft., 2 in.
Width:	10 ft., 6 in.
Height:	12 ft., 7 in.
Weight (maximum take-off):	21,000 lbs.
Cruising speed:	184 mph
Maximum altitude:	21,000 ft.
Range:	300 miles
Date of first flight:	1975

Left: In the tank-busting role, the AH-64A Apache can operate alone or in pairs. When working together, one Apache designates the target with its laser while the other fires its Hellfire missiles. Right: This view shows the TADS/PNVS (target acquisition-designation sight/pilot's night vision sensor) that enables the Apache to fly and fight in any weather, day or night.

112

Left: The Apache's power gives it the ability to hide behind terrain features such as hills and then quickly "pop up" to fire at enemy targets. **Right**: This Apache, on its way to maneuvers at dawn, carries 16 Hellfire missiles. The weapons operator is visible at his station.

BELL BOEING V-22 OSPREY

The V-22 Osprey is a hybrid, a cross between a helicopter and a fixed wing aircraft. Two gas turboshaft engines are mounted on the ends of wings attached to a conventional aircraft fuselage. To take off, the engines—with their three-bladed, 38-foot-diameter rotors—are rotated to point straight up. The aircraft rises vertically like a helicopter until the pilot rotates the engines into a horizontal position; the aircraft then flies like a conventional fixed wing aircraft. To land, the pilot rotates the engine pods to a position that enables the aircraft to land either like a helicopter or a VSL (very short landing) plane that uses only a minimal amount of runway. The aircraft cannot land like a typical fixed wing aircraft because the large rotor blades would actually hit the ground. The Osprey combines the vertical ascent/descent feature of the helicopter with the speed of conventional flight that helicopters cannot attain with the usual helicopter rotor design.

Development of the convertiplane concept began in the 1940s. By 1955, Bell had developed and flown the XV-3 convertiplane. In the XV-3, the entire wing rotated with the engines. Despite the project's success, there was no interest and the XV-3 went into limbo. In 1973, Bell responded to a NASA/Army proposal for an aircraft able to take off and land vertically but fly in a conventional mode with a new convertiplane design, the XV-15 (Bell designation Model 301). The XV-15, a smaller research version of the later V-22 Osprey, was the first to have only the engines rotate rather than the whole wing.

After Bell convinced the military and NASA of the viability of the tilt rotor concept, the United States Navy and the United States Air Force teamed up to develop the Joint Services Advanced Vertical Lift Aircraft. The first contracts were awarded in 1983 to both Bell and Boeing. Further contracts were given for design and development as well as for the construction of six flying and three static testing prototypes. The V-22 Osprey made its first successful flight in 1989, and the first deliveries are scheduled to go to the United States Marine Corps in 1991. However, attempts to reduce the federal budget deficit may stretch out production of the V-22 Osprey.

Since the Osprey will go first to the Marine Corps, the aircraft will have to operate from a variety of aircraft carriers and assault ships. The Navy requires the aircraft to be able to fold up and go below deck in less than 90 seconds. To meet that requirement, the Osprey has blades that fold on each hub and engine pods that tilt forward. The wings and engines can then be rotated to lie fore and aft, turning the craft into a compact box shape.

The Osprey will play a sizable role in the Marine Corps' over-the-horizon assault capability. The Air Force will use the Osprey for special operations and search and rescue. The Navy envisions the Osprey, with its longer range and hover time compared with a helicopter, playing a major role in antisubmarine warfare. The Army plans to use the Osprey for multirole transport and medevac.

The tilt rotor concept has wide potential application in civil aviation. In heavily populated urban areas where open land is either at a premium or nonexistent, concerns about the location of major airports continue. Although a civilian version of the Osprey probably will not replace the modern long-range jetliner, it could ease airport problems and

114

Left: The Bell Boeing V-22 Osprey lifts off on its first flight at Bell's Flight Research Center in Arlington, Texas. **Right:** The engine pods on the end of either wing can rotate up to allow the Osprey to take off like a helicopter and then forward for level flight.

have a profound effect on short and intermediate trips. The Osprey could reduce airports in urban areas to parking-lot size because of its ability to take off and land vertically with large numbers of passengers.

The Osprey is powered by two Allison T406-400 turboshaft engines each producing 6,000 horsepower. The engines turn large-diameter, changeable-pitch propellers/rotors in opposite directions, eliminating torque. The engines are mounted at the ends of high-mounted wings that are swept slightly forward. The two engines are linked by drive shafts so if one engine fails, the other will continue to turn both propellers.

The main cabin, or cargo hold, is 24 feet long by six feet wide. In the transport version, the V-22 Osprey can handle up to 24 fully equipped soldiers and two gunners, 5,700 pounds of cargo, or 12 stretcher casualties and assistance personnel. At the rear, the aircraft has a full-width ramp door. The pilot and copilot sit side by side in the conventional cockpit and located behind them is a jump seat for the third crew member. The aircraft has a digital fly-by-wire system developed by General Electric Corp. The fuselage, which is of conventional monocoque construction, is built by Boeing Helicopter Company. Grumman Aircraft builds the tail assembly and Bell the wings, drive system, and propeller/rotors.

Deployment of the Osprey with the military and entry into civil aviation should revolutionize short-range air transport and intercity air travel.

BELL BOEING V-22 OSPREY	
Main rotor diameter:	38 ft. (both)
Length:	57 ft., 4 in.
Width:	15 ft., 2.5 in.
Height:	17 ft., 4 in.
Weight (maximum take-off):	47,500 lbs. (vertical)
Cruising speed:	391 mph
Maximum altitude:	Not available
Range:	2,418 miles
Date of first flight:	1989

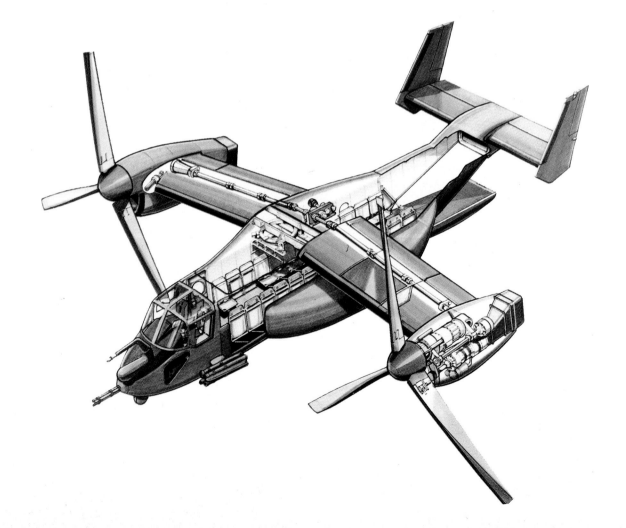

Left: This artist's cutaway of the Bell Boeing Osprey shows the control linkages that allow the Osprey's engines to rotate. Also seen is the cargo space/seating arrangement in the fuselage. Although armament is not planned, the illustration shows the Osprey with a 30mm chain gun in the nose and Hellfire missile launchers. **Right:** The V-22 Osprey, with its ability to take off and land vertically, will revolutionize short-haul air transport between cities.

KAMOV KA-25 HORMONE

The Kamov design bureau, named after its first director, aviation pioneer Nicholas Kamov, reached back to pre-World War II helicopter experimentation for the Soviet Navy's premier helicopter, the Ka-25 (NATO code-named, Hormone). The bureau selected the coaxial, twin rotor Gyroplan Laboratorie design developed by the two French pioneers, Breguet and Dorand. The counterrotating blades eliminated torque and permitted a highly compact design for shipboard use.

The development of the Ka-25 proceeded through the Ka-8 and Ka-10 helicopters, which were developed for reconnaissance and over-the-horizon targeting missions. In many respects, the Ka-8 and Ka-10 were similar to the Flettner FL 282 Kolibri, which the Germans had used against the Soviet Navy in the Baltic Sea during World War II. These early helicopters were followed by the larger Ka-15 and Ka-18, but these two helicopters, although similar in appearance to the Ka-25, never saw widespread service.

The Ka-15 and Ka-18 had been powered by piston engines, but the new Ka-25 helicopter, first flown in 1960, used twin Glushenkov GTD-3 gas turbine engines that nominally delivered 900 horsepower each. The GTD-3 was one of the first successful turboshaft engines produced in the Soviet Union. The turboshaft engines made the Ka-25 more than four times heavier and a great deal more powerful than its predecessors. The engines have since been up-rated to the 990 horsepower GTD-3BM. Each engine has its own fuel tank and plumbing. The use of two engines, rather than a single larger one, provides an added safety factor for over-the-water operations.

The coaxial counterrotating main rotors not only allow a more compact craft but also provide additional lift and speed because as one blade moves away from the oncoming airstream, thus losing lift, the opposite blade approaches the oncoming airstream, gaining lift. The main rotors are stacked one above the other on a double shaft; one shaft turns inside the other. This arrangement requires a complicated swash plate hinging system to cope with the clockwise/counterclockwise spinning of the rotors. Long push/pull rods are also needed to control the pitch of the top rotor blades. The multiplicity of hinges calls for close attention to lubrication. The original aluminum and honeycomb blades have been replaced by all-composite blades. The pilot can fold all six blades automatically.

The twin turboshaft engines allowed the Kamov designers flexibility to develop a utility helicopter for shipboard use that could be fitted for varying missions. Since the counterrotating blades eliminate torque, there is no need for a tail rotor, and the Kamov designers developed a boxy fuselage. The fuselage is covered with aluminum sandwich panels or sheets. The Ka-25's tail plane consists of a single vertical tail fin reaching above and below the stubby tail boom and two horizontal tail planes with vertical stabilizers on the end. These vertical stabilizers are canted inward at the top.

The cockpit holds the pilot and copilot and is mounted ahead of the cargo hold, which is 11 feet 6 inches long, 4 feet 9 inches wide, but only 4 feet 1 inch high. The low height is caused by a deep bay running the length of the fuselage beneath the floor that houses fuel tanks and equipment. Both pilot and copilot have sliding doors beside their seats, and the cargo hold has a single large sliding door. Depending on the mission and equipment, three to four additional crew members or up to 12 fully equipped troops can be carried in the cargo hold. Four wheels mounted on hydraulically damped struts form the landing gear. Each wheel can be fitted with buoyancy floats that can be inflated instantly with air bottles. The landing gear struts can be pivoted back against the fuselage to allow the crew an unobstructed view when towing antisubmarine warfare (ASW) equipment or when using their search radar.

The Hormone has appeared in three versions. The A model, which is used for ASW missions, is based on Kresta II- and Kara-class cruisers, Krivak III-class missile frigates, and the helicopter carriers *Moskva* and *Leningrad*. The A version carries an I/J frequency search band radar, sonobuoys, radar altimeter, doppler radar, autopilot controls, and various radio sets for communication with the fleet. It is also armed with 45 centimeter submarine torpedoes. Some A versions carry small air-to-surface guided missiles and perhaps wire-guided torpedoes. The B model, armed with cruise missiles, is used for anti-ship surveillance and targeting. It carries extensive radar equipment for locating, identifying, and targeting ships. The C model performs search and rescue and transport missions. This version lacks the electronics of the A and B models. Depending on the circumstances of a rescue or transport mission, the C model may be armed with at least 12.7 millimeter machine guns.

The Ka-25 Hormone, which reached the Soviet fleet in 1965, is beginning to show its age and lack of capability. Hormones are slowly being retired in favor of the newer and more capable Ka-27 Helix. The Ka-25 is still in use in the Indian Navy, the Syrian Air Force, Yugoslavia, and Vietnam.

KAMOV KA-25 HORMONE	
Rotor diameter:	51 ft., 7.75 in. (both)
Length:	32 ft.
Width:	12 ft., 4 in.
Height:	17 ft., 7.5 in.
Weight (maximum take-off):	16,535 lbs.
Cruising speed:	120 mph
Maximum altitude:	11,000 ft.
Range:	250 miles
Date of first flight:	1960

A Soviet Kamov Ka-25, which has just taken off from a Kresta-class cruiser, on an antisubmarine warfare mission near the Hawaiian Islands.

MIL MI-2 HOPLITE

The Mi-2, NATO codenamed Hoplite, is a small, single main rotor general-purpose helicopter used in the civilian and military roles. Because of its versatility, the Hoplite might well be characterized as the UH-1 Huey of the Soviet Union and Warsaw Pact military forces.

In the late 1950s, the Mil design bureau decided to up-rate its Mi-4 general-purpose helicopter by replacing the piston engine with gas turbine engines. The result, the Mi-8 Hip, was so successful that the Mil bureau undertook to do the same with its general-purpose Mi-1 Hare. The single piston engine was replaced by two Isotov GTD-350 turbo-shaft engines that produced 400 horsepower each. Together, the two engines yielded 40 percent more power than the single piston engine at a penalty of only 50 percent more weight. This effectively doubled the maximum load that the Hoplite could lift compared with the Hare. Hoplites built after 1986 are powered by 444-horsepower Isotov GTD-350P engines.

The Mi-2 made its first flight in September 1961. Except for a more hunchbacked appearance, which is caused by the larger fairing that covers the two gas turbine engines, the Mi-2 looks very much like its predecessor, the Mi-1. The Mi-2 also has two round air inlets that can be heated by hot air drawn from the engines to prevent icing of the inlets during Arctic or winter flying conditions. The Hoplite has a third air inlet between and above the turbine air inlets. A fan draws additional air through this inlet to cool the engine and transmission lubricating oil.

The Mi-2 Hoplite is the general-purpose helicopter of Soviet military forces, serving as a utility, scout, reconnaissance, and communications helicopter. More than 4,500 Mi-2 helicopters in various models have been sold throughout the world. Counted among its many customers are Poland, Czechoslovakia, Romania, and Cuba. The Hoplight has sold well because it is an inexpensive, relatively cheap aircraft. Although some aspects of its performance, particularly climbing ability, are unimpressive, the aircraft is well developed and can be configured to almost any conceivable role.

Although normally not armed, the Mi-2 Hoplite can carry either 57 millimeter free-flight rockets held in four pods, two mounted on either side on racks attached to the fuselage, or four AT-3 Sagger antitank guided missiles. Also, some Hoplites have been reported carrying a 23mm cannon mounted in a chin pod and a 12.7mm machine gun.

The main rotor is of a conventional construction and rotates counterclockwise, as is usual with most Mil bureau helicopters. The fully articulated hub carries three main blades that are built up around an aluminum-alloy spar and 20 aluminum or glass fiber pockets. For operation in winter or Arctic conditions, the blades contain electrically operated de-icers. The leading edges have flutter masses, and the trailing edges are equipped with tabs that can be adjusted only while the helicopter is on the ground. The landing gear is not retractable; the main wheels are mounted on struts on either side of the fuselage, and there is a twin-tired nose wheel.

The cockpit is mounted beneath the air inlets, and the pilot is seated on the left. The main cabin behind the cockpit is 7 feet 5 inches long, 4 feet 1 inch wide, and 4 feet 7 inches high. The Mi-2 can carry up to eight fully equipped troops, the equivalent of one infantry squad. With no passengers, the Hoplite can carry 1,543 pounds of cargo or four stretchers and a medic. The Hoplite can haul externally up to 1,764 pounds of cargo slung from its cargo hook. The fuselage is constructed of a light alloy. Although the aft section of the fuselage sweeps sharply upward to the tail boom, there is no rear-opening door to the main cabin. Entry is gained through doors located on both sides just behind the cockpit. Fuel is carried in a rubber bladder beneath the main floor, as in many Mil bureau designs. Two auxiliary fuel tanks, each holding 52.4 gallons, can be mounted on the weapons racks.

The avionics of the Hoplite are conventional and include radar altimeter, HF and VHF radio, gyro compass, and radio compass. Although military versions are believed to carry a sight for guiding antitank missiles, most Hoplites have no advanced combat equipment and are used for transport, general utility, and communications.

The Mi-2 Hoplite is a Soviet-designed helicopter used widely throughout the Soviet military and about 675 now serve with military ground forces. But it has never been built in the Soviet Union. The Mi-2, as with most Soviet light and general aviation aircraft, is built in Poland at the PZL factory, which was known as the WSK works until 1966.

MIL MI-2 HOPLITE	
Main rotor diameter:	47 ft., 6.9 in.
Tail rotor diameter:	8 ft., 10.25 in.
Length:	37 ft., 4 in.
Width:	Not available
Height:	12 ft., 3.6 in.
Weight (maximum take-off):	7,826 lbs.
Cruising speed:	118 mph
Maximum altitude:	3,280 ft.
Range:	105 miles
Date of first flight:	1961

MIL MI-14 HAZE

Except for the shorter fuselage and longer tail boom, the Mi-14, NATO codenamed Haze, somewhat resembles the SH-3 Sea King. Both helicopters have boat-shaped hulls for on-the-water operations and turboshaft engines mounted atop the fuselage. The Sea King's tail rotor is mounted to the left, the Mi-14's to the right.

The Mi-14 Haze derives from the Mi-8/Mi-17 Hip series of helicopters; it was developed as a shore-based antisubmarine warfare helicopter to replace the aging Mi-4. The Haze uses the same TV3-117A turboshaft engines as the Mi-17 Hip-H and the Mi-24 Hind. Overall, the Haze and the Hip-H aircraft are quite similar. Except for the boat-like hull, the Haze has the same lines and appearance as the Mi-17 Hip-H.

Although the hull of the Mi-14 is watertight, on-the-water operations are not expected to be a normal part of its operations. Even with the main rotor turning, the hull—which contains two weapons bays that extend nearly the entire length of the fuselage—and the round radome—protective housing for radar antennae mounted under the nose—would render the craft relatively unstable in all but a dead calm sea. The main landing gear and the two nose wheels located on either side of the fuselage are fully retractable.

The Mi-14 Haze-A is configured as an antisubmarine warfare craft with a crew of four or five. It carries sonobuoys, flares, dye and smoke markers, the standard Soviet 407 millimeter antisubmarine torpedo, depth charges, and mines. In addition to the sur-

face-scanning radar mounted in the dome beneath the nose, the Haze carries a doppler radar mounted under the tail boom just aft of the fuselage, a sonar unit in a retractable dome under the fuselage, dipping sonar, and a towable magnetic anomaly detector housed in a pod at the rear of the fuselage. When not deployed, the magnetic anomaly detector is stored at an upward angle of about 40 degrees, making it look somewhat like an abbreviated tail.

The Mi-14 Haze-B is the mine-countermeasures version. It mounts two equipment storage pods under the tail boom on either side of the doppler radar pod. A long fairing that extends the length of the right side of the Haze probably carries additional fuel.

The Mi-14 Haze-C is flown by Poland and the Soviet Union as a search and rescue helicopter. This version can be identified by the searchlights that are mounted on either side of the nose, the retractable rescue hoist, and a large sliding door on the left side behind the cockpit.

The Mi-14 Haze made its first flight in 1973. It is used by the Soviet Navy from shore-based installations, and it is also in use with Bulgarian, Cuban, Libyan, North Korean, East German, Romanian, and Polish military services.

This Soviet Mi-14, equipped for naval service, carries a magnetic anomaly detector, visible at the rear of the fuselage.

MIL MI-14 HAZE	
Main rotor diameter:	69 ft., 10.25 in.
Tail rotor diameter:	12 ft., 9.9 in.
Length:	60 ft., 5.4 in.
Width:	8 ft., 2.5 in.
Height:	22 ft., 7.75 in.
Weight (maximum take-off):	28,660 lbs.
Cruising speed:	143 mph
Maximum altitude:	16,400 ft.
Range:	575 miles
Date of first flight:	1973

The Mil Mi-8, NATO codenamed Hip, is the most numerous transport helicopter in the military services of the Soviet Union, Warsaw Pact nations, and Soviet client states. The Hip is found in service on every inhabited continent except Australia and North America. First produced in 1961, it is still in production in an up-rated, more powerful version, the Mi-17, NATO codenamed Hip-H.

The Mi-8 is a transport helicopter with two gas turbine engines that was originally developed from the Mil Mi-4, which was powered by a piston engine. In the West, the Mi-4 was at first mistakenly considered a copy of the Sikorsky H-19 Chickasaw, but the Mi-4 was in fact about three times more powerful. When Mil designers added two gas turbine engines to an improved Mi-4 airframe, they had developed an extremely powerful and versatile helicopter. If a comparison were to be made with a Western helicopter design, the Mil Mi-8 would be broadly similar to the Sikorsky S-61/SH-3 Sea King.

The Mi-8 is powered by two Isotov TV2-117A turboshaft engines developing 1,700 horsepower each. Both engines are mounted above the main cabin/cargo hold area, and the air inlets extend forward to the rear of the cockpit.

The main rotor is five-bladed. The blades are constructed of a single hollow main spar of extruded aluminum alloy and 21 separate pieces of honeycomb construction bolted to the main spar. The main rotor is equipped with standard de-icing equipment. The tail rotor has three blades, which are manufactured in a manner similar to the main rotor's blades. On the Mi-8, the tail rotor is mounted on the right side at the end of the tail boom.

The fuselage is conventional semi-monocoque construction. The tail rotor mounting serves as a vertical stabilizer, and two horizontal stabilizers project from either side of the tail boom just ahead of the tail rotor. The landing gear follows the usual Soviet pattern: The nose wheel is mounted beneath the aft end of the cockpit, and the main landing gear wheels are set on struts projecting from the fuselage. All wheels are nonretractable. Additional fuel tanks can be mounted on either side of the fuselage. The right auxiliary fuel tank is longer than the left tank to allow the main cabin door to open.

In the cockpit, the pilot and copilot sit side by side and located directly behind them is a jump seat for the flight engineer. The cockpit and main cabin can be air-conditioned or heated, but separate equipment must be installed for either function. The main cabin can be configured for cargo or for passengers. In the military version, 24 tip-up seats line each wall. The civilian version can carry up to 28 passengers in seats mounted four abreast. The civilian helicopter can be differentiated from the military helicopter by the cabin windows. The civilian Hip features large rectangular windows, while the military Hip has round windows with ports that allow troops to fire their weapons during the landing phase of an assault. The military version carries a winch, and the floor has either rings or tie-down bolts for securing cargo. All Mi-8s can be reconfigured for medevac missions and can carry 12 stretchers with provision for medical personnel. The rear clamshell doors in the military version allow for the quick loading of small vehicles and bulky weapons.

The Mi-8 Hip-E is perhaps the most heavily armed helicopter in the world. The Hip-E was designed and built primarily for the assault role. Armament includes a 12.7 millimeter DShK heavy machine gun mounted in the nose beneath the cockpit and aimed from the cockpit. The Hip-E also carries up to 192 57mm free-flight rockets in six rocket launchers. Three launchers are mounted on each side on armament racks projecting from the side of the fuselage. Two AT-2 Swatter guided missiles per rack can also be mounted above the 57mm rocket pods. Other armament observed on the Hip-E include napalm bombs, general-purpose bombs, and butterfly antipersonnel bombs. After the Afghan resistance fighters were armed with British Blowpipe and American Stinger one-man, portable antiaircraft missiles, the Hip, as well as all other Soviet aircraft, were quickly fitted with chaff and flare dispensers. The export version of the Mi-8 is configured to carry the AT-3 Sagger antitank guided missile, which is not as sophisticated as the AT-2 Swatter.

The Mi-17 Hip-H is a more powerful version of the Mi-8. It uses two Isotov TV3-117MT turboshaft engines that each produce 1,900 horsepower. The same engines are used in the Mi-14 Haze and the Mi-24 Hind. Deflectors protect the engines from ingesting sand or other foreign matter during field operations. The Mi-17 has been described as an amalgamation of two aircraft, the airframe of the Mi-8 and the engines of the Mi-24. The Mi-17 has shorter engine air inlets than the Mi-8, and the tail rotor is mounted on the left side of the tail boom. There is little else in appearance to distinguish the Mi-8 from the Mi-17. The extra power provided by the new engines was needed to offset the increased weight of new armor and the addition of a GSh-23 23mm multibarrel gun system. The Mi-17 has also received improvements in avionics and control systems. An auxiliary power unit was added to start the engines in remote areas.

The number of variations of the Mi-8 can be confusing. The Mi-8 Hip-A was the single-engine prototype, and the Hip-B was the twin-engine prototype. The Mi-8 Hip-C became the basic production configuration, best known as an assault transport. The Hip-D is configured for a communications role and can be identified by the additional electronics antennae and rectangular boxes mounted on the external racks. The Mi-8 Hip-E is the current standard assault helicopter in Soviet service; it is the most heavily armed of the

The Mi-8 Hip C was the forerunner of the Mi-24 Hind D. This Hip C is equipped to carry folding-fin rockets and AT-2 Sagger missiles.

Mi-8 series. The Hip-F is similar to the Hip-E but is reserved for export; accordingly, armament and avionics will vary from customer to customer. The Hip-G is an up-rated communications helicopter with doppler radar. The Hip-H is also known as the Mi-17 Hip-H, discussed earlier. The Hip-J and Hip-K are used for communications jamming. The K model can be identified by the large array of usualshaped Yagi-type antennae mounted on either side of the fuselage.

The Mi-8/Mi-17 series is one of the most successful military helicopters ever. More than 10,000 of the two versions combined have been built. They serve in the armed forces and civil aviation components of at least 39 nations. More than 2,400 Mi-8s and Mi-17s are currently part of 20 helicopter attack regiments that support Soviet ground forces in the field. Each regiment has up to 60 Mi-8/17s or Mi-24s.

MIL MI-8 HIP/MI-17 HIP-H	
Main rotor diameter:	69 ft., 10.25 in.
Tail rotor diameter:	12 ft., 9.9 in.
Length:	Mi-8: 59 ft., 7.4 in.
	Mi-17: 60 ft., 5.4 in.
Width:	8 ft., 2.5 in.
Height:	18 ft., 6.5 in.
Weight (maximum take-off):	Mi-8: 26,455 lbs.
	Mi-17: 28,660 lbs.
Cruising speed:	140 mph
Maximum altitude:	Mi-8: 14,760 ft.
	Mi-17: 16,400 ft.
Range:	Mi-8: 289 miles
	Mi-17: 307 miles
Date of first flight:	1962

Left: The chief engineer of a collective farm and the pilot of an Mi-8 discuss the route the helicopter will take while fertilizing the farm's fields. Right: Aeroflot uses helicopters like these Mi-8 Hips to reach such remote regions of the USSR as this mountain village of Aibga in the Krasnodar territory.

MIL MI-24 HIND

The Mi-24, NATO codenamed Hind, has been subject to a number of misinterpretations. It has been characterized as a flying tank, as a gunship, and as an armed troop transport. In fact, it is all of these and more.

The Mi-24 was designed as an armed troop transport to follow on the Mi-8 Hip series. The Soviet Army, after studying American experiences in South Vietnam, recognized a need for a troop transport that could provide its own ground suppression fire. The first version of the Mi-24, the Hind-A, was heavily armed with pods containing 57 millimeter rockets, the AT-2 Swatter antitank missile, and 12.7mm machine guns. The main compartment behind the cockpit could hold up to eight fully equipped troops, a full infantry squad, who were trained to fire their weapons through portholes when landing in a hot combat zone. These design parameters made the Mi-24 Hind-A a very large helicopter and therefore more vulnerable to ground fire than Western designers thought necessary.

The Hind-A carried a crew of three: pilot, copilot/weapons operator, and flight engineer. The pilot and copilot/weapons operator sat side by side in a roomy cockpit that was armored for protection against small arms ground fire. The fuselage was conventional semi-monocoque construction. A series of bumps, protrusions, and blisters projecting from the streamlined fuselage provided mountings or shields for a variety of electronic and optical sights, target designators, and communications gear. The Hind's tricycle landing gear was fully retractable.

Two TV2-117A turboshaft engines, the same engines used in the Mi-8 Hip, were mounted atop the main fuselage with an oil cooler bolted on top of the engine. A small auxiliary power unit was set behind the oil cooler and the main rotor.

The main rotor was similar to but smaller than that used in the Mi-8/Mi-17 series. Main rotor blades were made from titanium spars and honeycomb cores covered with glass fiber. A leading edge electric de-icer and anti-erosion strip were included. Balance tabs were found on the trailing edge of all five blades. The tail rotor was mounted on the right side of the swept-back vertical stabilizer, and the tail rotor blades were of aluminum alloy.

Two wings provided nearly one-quarter of the Hind's lift, improving performance over that of the Mi-8/Mi-17. The wings provided mountings for the variety of weapons the Hind was able to carry and were bent downward to make weapons loading easier.

The Mi-24 Hind-A was deployed to Soviet Army squadrons in East Germany beginning in 1974 to patrol the border between East and West Germany. Experience gained there, and supplemented by battle experience in Afghanistan, led to substantial changes in equipment, mission, and tactics.

The Hind-D was the result. It is quite similar to the A model except for two major changes. More powerful TV3-117A engines, producing 2,200 horsepower each, were substituted, and the tail rotor was mounted on the left side of the vertical stabilizer to reduce noise. The cockpit was redesigned to meet the needs of its new mission, which is to serve as a flying tank, or gunship. The pilot and copilot/weapons operator no longer sat side by side but rather in tandem with the pilot behind and above the copilot/weapons operator for better all-around visibility. The copilot/weapons operator's station was up-rated with more extensive instrumentation and improved targeting devices. Both crew positions were heavily armored and given their own separate canopies. A four barrel 12.7mm Gatling-type machine gun was mounted in the nose, giving the Hind-D an air-to-air, as well as an air-to-surface, capability. The ability to carry the eight-member infantry squad was retained.

The immediate follow-on to the D model was the Hind-E. The E model was given wingtip launchers and four pylons under the wings that enabled it to carry and launch up to 12 AT-6 Spiral radio-controlled guided missiles. The Hind-F is similar to the Hind-E, but it carries a 30mm twin barrel cannon on the right side of the fuselage. Both versions can carry spare missiles and machine gun ammunition in the main cabin.

The Mi-24's avionics include VHF and UHF radios, autopilot, radar altimeter, blind-flying instrumentation, automated navigation/map display systems, and in the D and E variations, an effective low-light television camera and receiver system for night operations. The D and E also have a forward-looking infrared targeting system.

The Hind was king of the hill in Afghanistan until the introduction of one-man anti-aircraft missiles like the British Blowpipe and the American Stinger. To counter the infrared-seeking Stinger and Blowpipe, infrared suppressors were mounted on the engine exhausts, and chaff and flare dispensers were made more effective.

More than 2,400 Mi-24 Hinds in various configurations have been built, and production continues at the rate of about 15 per month. An export version of the Mi-24, a less capable model called the Mi-25, has been sold to Soviet client states.

MIL MI-24 HIND-D	
Main rotor diameter:	55 ft., 9 in.
Tail rotor diameter:	12 ft., 9.5 in.
Length:	57 ft., 5 in.
Width:	6.5 ft. (estimated)
Height:	21 ft., 4 in.
Weight (maximum take-off):	24,250 lbs.
Cruising speed:	183 mph
Maximum altitude:	14,750 ft.
Range:	198 miles
Date of first flight:	1972

The Mi-24D is the most heavily armed and armored helicopter gunship now flying. While fighting in Afghanistan, Soviet pilots worked out defensive tactics against one-man antiaircraft missiles like the Stinger and the Blowpipe.

KAMOV KA-27 HELIX

It is not clear which came first, the military version or the civilian version of the helicopter codenamed Helix by NATO. The military version is designated Ka-27, the civilian version, Ka-32. The military Helix first appeared in photographs taken of the *Udaloy*, a new Soviet antisubmarine guided missile destroyer, during 1981 fleet exercises in the Baltic Sea. Two Ka-27s were positioned on the stern of the *Udaloy*. The civilian version was first shown during a scientific conference at Minsk in the same year.

What is clear is that the Ka-27 Helix is a much more capable helicopter than its predecessor, the Ka-25 Hormone. Like the Hormone, the Helix uses the counterrotating coaxial, three-bladed main rotors that are the trademark of Soviet ship-based helicopters. The Helix's blades appear to be made of composite materials, and the rotor hubs are of titanium and steel. In both civilian and military versions, the six blades can be manually folded to the rear.

Helicopters with coaxial, counterrotating blades characteristically produce vibrations that increase the need for maintenance and decrease aircraft life. According to descriptive material published in the Soviet Union, the Helix's main rotor system has been designed to reduce vibration. To help minimize vibration, the main rotor shaft is attached to the aircraft by straps and adjustable weights are attached to the lower rotors.

The Helix, which is quite similar in design to the Hormone, can be differentiated from the Hormone by the long, smoother engine fairing on either side of the top of the fuselage and the absence of the central vertical fin above and below the stubby tail boom. The Helix also has a more rounded cockpit canopy that flares into the nose, whereas the Hormone has a narrow wind screen that forms a step where it meets the nose. More titanium has been used in the Helix to reduce overall weight, and special attention has been paid to making the helicopter resistant to corrosion to lengthen its service life in the salt-filled marine environment.

The 990 horsepower Glushenkov GTD-3 gas turbine engines have been exchanged for two 2,225 horsepower Isotov TV3-117V turboshaft engines—similar to those used in the Mi-24 Hind. These engines provide the Helix with greater speed and payload capacity than its predecessor. As with the Hormone, should engine trouble develop, the Helix can fly on only one engine.

The Helix can carry up to 8,818 pounds inside its cargo hold or 11,022 pounds slung beneath the helicopter on its cargo hook. Indeed, one of the reasons for building the Ka-32 civilian version was to have a "compact truck" for hauling cargo and earth-moving equipment into remote areas. The Helix's cargo hold/main cabin is 2 feet longer but slightly narrower and lower than the Hormone's; thus, the Helix can carry 16 passengers instead of 12. A sliding door is located on the left side of the main cabin, and a smaller emergency door is located on the right. Despite its greater capacity and lengthened fuselage, the Helix can still fit into the deck space and hangar accommodations used by the Ka-25 Hormone.

When serving in the transport and utility role, the Ka-27 Helix normally carries a minimum crew of three. The pilot (on the left) and copilot, or navigator in the civilian Ka-32, are seated side by side. The third crew member sits behind the copilot/navigator. Behind the pilot and copilot/navigator are two sliding doors that divide the cockpit from the main cabin/cargo hold. The cockpit is air-conditioned.

A great deal of attention has been paid to automating the helicopter's controls. For antisubmarine warfare (ASW) operations, the new autopilot can provide an automatic approach and hover. The Helix also automatically maintains constant rotor thrust during turns, which aids the pilot significantly when landing on a heaving deck in rough seas.

The Helix is built in four basic configurations. The Helix A, based aboard ships of the Soviet Navy, is used for ASW and has been operational since 1982. The Helix B is used as an infantry assault transport and is deployed on ships of the Ivan Rogov-class of amphibious assault ships. The Helix C, also known as the Ka-32, is the civil aviation version. The Ka-27 Helix D is used for search and rescue and for plane guard duties; it has been observed deployed on Kiev-class aircraft carriers. An export version of the Ka-27 Helix, dubbed the Ka-28, has been purchased by Yugoslavia. The Indian Navy has ordered eight Ka-28s.

No armament data for the Ka-27 Helix has been released to the public by either the Soviets or NATO, but it is likely that the Ka-27A carries at least the same armament as the Ka-25 Hormone. The Helix is probably also capable of carrying an assortment of homing torpedoes, air-to-surface guided missiles, depth charges, and naval mines. The B model, used in the assault transport role, and the D model, used for certain search and rescue missions, would each carry at a minimum 12.7 millimeter machine guns.

KAMOV KA-27 HELIX	
Rotor diameter:	52 ft., 2 in. (both)
Length:	37 ft., 1 in.
Width:	13 ft., 1.5 in.
Height:	17 ft., 8.5 in.
Weight (maximum take-off):	27,775 lbs.
Cruising speed:	155 mph
Maximum altitude:	19,685 ft.
Range:	497 miles
Date of first flight:	1978 or 1979

The Kamov Ka-27 Helix has much better antisubmarine warfare capabilities compared with the earlier Ka-25 Hormone.

MIL MI-28 HAVOC

As of mid-1989, the Mi-28 Havoc had not yet made its appearance. Western intelligence sources, both classified and open, have been predicting the imminent deployment of the Havoc since the early 1980s. Only a few photographs and illustrations are available. The most detailed illustration is a United States Department of Defense artist's rendering that seems less and less accurate as time goes on. Most sources infer that the Mi-28, NATO codenamed Havoc, is still in prototype testing, but the Defense Department seems to think it could be fielded in late 1989 or 1990.

The great number of helicopters lost to one-man antiaircraft guided missiles in Afghanistan between 1985 and 1988 could possibly be responsible for the delay in introducing the new Mi-28 Havoc. Soviet designers may be seeking new ways to decrease the helicopter's vulnerability to these deadly weapons. Most likely, the new generation of Soviet helicopters will either stand off at some distance or pop up from cover to fire its weapons, rather than orbit the battlefield while delivering assault fire.

Since the Defense Department probably obtained the information on which to base their illustration of the Mi-28 from actual photographs taken by satellites or reconnaissance aircraft, it seems reasonable to assume that the major details are correct. Other inferences can be drawn from published information.

To start, one of the Mi-24 Hind's greatest drawbacks in combat was its excessive width, which made it a large target for antiaircraft guns and missiles. *Jane's All The World's Aircraft* (1987–88 edition) and the United States Air Force Association's most recent survey of Soviet military aircraft suggest that the Mi-28 will be confined to the ground assault role. If so, it will not need to carry troops, and the wide main cabin can be eliminated. If the tandem cockpit design is retained, which it surely will be, the fuselage would be reduced to almost half the width of the Mi-24 Hind-A.

Most sources seem to think that the Havoc will use the Isotov TV3-117 turboshaft engines, which also power the Mi-24 Hind-C/D/E and the Mi-17 Hip-H. This would be consistent with previous Mil bureau design practice. The two engines would be slung in pods on either side of an extension of the cockpit/main rotor fairing at the top of the fuselage. The exhausts are angled upward but not fitted with infrared suppressors. But combat-ready Mi-28 helicopters would certainly use infrared suppressors. The engine air intakes would likely be fitted with the flattened, cone-shaped dust deflectors developed by the Mil bureau.

The Havoc has stubby wings that slant downward, as is the case with the Mi-24, that would provide as much as 25 percent of total lift. The Mi-28 Havoc's wings are swept back, which suggests a higher operating speed than the Mi-24. The Mi-28 will also be fitted with weapons attaching points similar to those used on the Mi-24 Hind-D/E.

The cockpit will probably duplicate the layout found in the Mi-24 except that the pilot and copilot/weapons operator positions will be set further back from the nose. The extra room will be used to house electronics and radar. It is likely that the separate armor-protected crew positions will be retained. The canopy will most likely be nonreflective, flat glass.

Jane's suggests that a new design for the main and tail rotors will be used but provides no details. The Air Force Association survey states only that it is new. All pictures and information suggest that the Mi-28 Havoc will have a swept-back vertical stabilizer crossed at the top with a horizontal stabilizer. The tail rotor—probably three-bladed—will be mounted at the end of the horizontal stabilizer on the right side.

All pictures, from whatever source, show the Mi-28 Havoc armed with a large caliber, multibarrel gun mounted in a pod slung beneath the helicopter's nose. The gun will probably be the GSh 23 millimeter or 30mm, which would provide the helicopter with significant air-to-air capability. The Havoc will at least equal, if not surpass, the Mi-24 in weapons-carrying ability. The wings suggest there is room for up to 16 AT-6 Spiral radio/laser-guided antitank missiles, or eight AT-6s and four to eight air-to-air guided missiles, or 64 57mm air-to-ground rockets.

The appearance in military service of the Mi-28 Havoc is only a matter of time. When it is deployed, the Soviets will have gained an edge in ground assault helicopters that the West will have to counter.

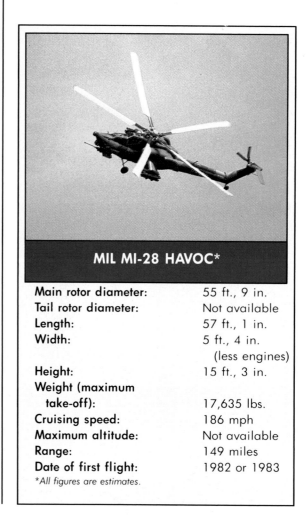

MIL MI-28 HAVOC*

Main rotor diameter:	55 ft., 9 in.
Tail rotor diameter:	Not available
Length:	57 ft., 1 in.
Width:	5 ft., 4 in. (less engines)
Height:	15 ft., 3 in.
Weight (maximum take-off):	17,635 lbs.
Cruising speed:	186 mph
Maximum altitude:	Not available
Range:	149 miles
Date of first flight:	1982 or 1983

*All figures are estimates.

Left: The Mi-28 Havoc is the Soviet Union's latest gunship. Introduction was delayed several years to allow the lessons learned in Afghanistan to be incorporated into the aircraft's design. **Right:** The Mi-28 Havoc is a smaller and vastly improved edition of the Mi-24 Hind.

KAMOV KA-36 HOKUM

The Kamov Ka-36, NATO codenamed Hokum, is reputed to be the first of a new breed of military helicopters designed primarily for air-to-air combat. As with the Mi-28 Havoc, the imminent deployment of the Ka-36 Hokum has been rumored for years. Only illustrations of the Hokum exist in the open press. While there have been reports of the Havoc flying in Afghanistan, no such reports concerning the Hokum have been made. The fact of the Hokum's existence has been published in *Soviet Military Power*, the annual report by the United States Department of Defense on the state of Soviet military forces, since the 1984 edition. An artist's rendering, believed to be accurate, has been included since the 1987 edition. From the drawings and the few published reports (such as *Jane's All The World's Aircraft*) that contain hard data, it is possible to draw the following conclusions about the Ka-36 Hokum.

The Hokum will be extremely fast for a helicopter, with a speed in excess of 215 miles per hour. This speed is achieved by streamlining the fuselage to a greater degree than past Soviet helicopters and by using quite large wings in proportion to the overall size of the aircraft. These wings could provide as much as 35 to 45 percent of total lift.

In the drawings, the Hokum is shown with a coaxial counterrotating main rotor. The main rotor system will probably be similar, at least in outward appearances, to the coaxial counterrotating main rotors used by the Kamov design bureau in the past. The rotor could be particularly close to the one developed for the Ka-27/32 Helix. If so, then the main rotor will consist of two sets of fully articulated three-bladed rotors with swept-back tips turning in opposite directions. The blades will be state-of-the-art carbon fiber and honeycomb construction and will probably use the adjustable tab system that the Kamov bureau favors.

Two gas turbine engines will be slung on either side of the fuselage, below the main rotor. It is possible these engines will be the same TV3-117 series of turboshaft engines that power the Ka-27/32, the Mi-24, and the Mi-28. The Hokum apparently uses a fixed wing aircraft-style tail assembly with conventional vertical and horizontal stabilizers. The Defense Department drawings show vertical plates at the ends of the horizontal stabilizer.

Judging from the size of the Hokum shown in the drawings, it will carry a crew of two: pilot and copilot/weapons operator. The pilot will sit behind and above the copilot/weapons operator. As in the Mi-24 Hind-D/E, the Hokum's cockpit will probably have separate armored compartments for each crew member. The cockpit will most likely be enclosed by an impact-resistant, flat plate canopy. Landing gear will be fully retractable.

The Department of Defense has stated in *Soviet Military Power* and other assessments of the Hokum that no Ka-36 has been observed carrying, or testing, antitank weaponry. Drawings show two guns. One gun, perhaps a 12.7 millimeter machine gun, protrudes from the left side of the streamlined nose. The other gun is possibly a 23mm or 30mm rapid-firing cannon and is mounted in a weapons pod on the right side of the aircraft below the cockpit. The extra-large wings would certainly provide ample hard point attachments for a range of weaponry from free-flight rockets to such air-to-air missiles as the AA-2 Atoll, the AA-8 Aphid, or the new AA-11 Archer.

As with the Mi-28 Havoc, production and deployment of the Ka-36 Hokum may have been delayed to incorporate lessons learned in Afghanistan. When this new air-to-air combat helicopter is finally introduced into regular service, the Soviets will have a tremendous edge along the forward edge of the battle area. In the West, the development of an air combat helicopter has lagged so far behind as to be nonexistent. The only work in this area has been half-hearted testing of the

American AH-64A Apache, the UH-60 Blackhawk, the AH-1W SuperCobra, the CH-53 Super Stallion, and the British Lynx 3 for air-to-air combat.

Almost any military helicopter that can handle the payload and associated electronics can be equipped with a rapid-firing cannon, machine guns, and air-to-air missiles. But this does not make a helicopter air-combat worthy any more than hanging weapons on a Cessna 180 would turn it into a fixed wing fighter. Clearly, the Hokum, with its expected speed and agility, will be *the* air-combat helicopter for some time to come. Upon starting production, the Department of Defense expects the "Hokum will give the Soviets a significant rotary-wing air superiority capability. The system has no current Western counterpart."

KAMOV KA-36 HOKUM*	
Main rotor diameter:	45 ft., 10 in.
Length:	44 ft., 3.5 in.
Width:	Not available
Height:	17 ft., 8 in.
Weight (maximum take-off):	16,500 lbs.
Cruising speed:	215 mph
Maximum altitude:	Not available
Range:	155 miles
Date of first flight:	Not available
*All figures are estimates.	

The Kamov Ka-36 Hokum is believed to represent a new generation of helicopter. To achieve greater speed, the Hokum uses a counter-rotating main rotor and has no tail rotor.

WESTLAND LYNX

Of the three helicopters that were part of the 1967 Anglo-French helicopter agreement—Puma, Gazelle, and Lynx—the Lynx was the only one to sport a British design. Built as a multirole general-purpose aircraft for the military and civilian marketplace, the Lynx quickly established itself as an agile aircraft capable of a variety of missions.

Over its long history, the Lynx has undergone many updates, upgrades, and modifications. Early models of the Lynx, the British Army AH 1, the British Navy HAS 2, and many export versions, were powered by two Rolls Royce Gem 2 turboshaft engines that develop up to 900 horsepower. Later export versions and most modern aircraft in the British Army or British Navy inventory now feature up-rated Gem 41-1 or 41-2 engines. These newer engines are considerably more powerful and produce either 1,120 horsepower or 1,315 horsepower.

Because the Lynx is a such a versatile helicopter, it performs many roles for both the military and civilian services. In the aircraft's basic configuration, the pilot and copilot are seated side by side, and optional dual controls are available. Normal carrying capacity is up to 10 combat soldiers or, in its medevac role, three stretchers and a medical attendant. The Lynx can haul up to 2,000 pounds of internal cargo or carry up to 3,000 pounds externally via a sling system.

The basic British Army version of the helicopter was called the AH Mark 1. Two up-rated versions have since been produced. The AH Mark 5 had more powerful engines; the AH Mark 7 sported the AH Mark 5's larger engines and also featured an improved tail rotor design with composite blades. The new tail rotor design not only reduced aircraft operating noise but also increased the aircraft's ability to hover for long periods of time while carrying high weight limits. For the anti-armor role, this increased hover time greatly enhanced the helicopter's ability to seek out, wait for, and then destroy tanks.

In the British Navy, the basic Lynx helicopter was called the HAS Mark 2 and was designed for antisubmarine warfare (ASW) duties. But both the British and French Navy versions perform many more missions and duties than simply seeking out and destroying enemy submarines. Lynx variants are capable of search and rescue, reconnaissance, fleet communication, airborne warfare coordination, troop transport, supply replenishment, fire control, and functioning as missile launch platforms for surface vessel warfare.

Differences between the army and naval versions for the most part can be found on the naval version, which has various shipborne features that include a beefed-up landing gear and different avionics, cockpit layout, and weapons systems. The aircraft's tail boom and main blades can be folded to make a more compact and easily stowable aircraft, a necessity on ships where space is at a premium.

The versatility of the Lynx allows it to carry a large variety and quantity of weapons systems. Naval versions with antisubmarine or antiship missions will carry one or more types of surface/dipping sonars, reconnaissance pods, sonobuoys, flares and markers, Sting Ray computer controlled torpedoes, Mark 44 homing torpedoes, Mark 11 depth charges, British Aerospace Sea Skua/Aerospatiale AS 15TT/IFV Penguin antiship missiles, 20 millimeter or 30mm cannons, machine gun pods, folding-fin rockets, and Stinger air-to-air missiles for fending off aerial attacks. The Army version of the Lynx offers an equally wide array of modern weapons systems. Among the armaments it carries are: up to eight TOW missiles with reloads, folding-fin rockets, 20mm or 30mm cannons

Left: A British Sea Lynx takes part in NATO exercises in March 1987. Right: The Lynx AH Mark 7 is the second up-rated version of the British Army's basic Lynx AH 1.

mounted either in the cabin or on the weapons pylons, two quadruple HOT or RBS-70 missile launchers, General Dynamics Stinger or Mata Mistral antiaircraft missiles, BAe (British Aerospace) Alarm antiradar missiles, machine gun pintle mounts or pod configuration, and a TV reconnaissance camera pod for battlefield surveillance.

Work on the Lynx continues; production is split between Westland, which shoulders 70 percent of the workload, and Aerospatiale, which carries 30 percent of the workload. More than 300 Lynx aircraft are in service worldwide. The new Super Lynx beginning to appear features extended range and load capabilities, additional weapons stores, new avionics and detection gear, and an all-weather day/night attack capability. The Super Lynx also has a more efficient tail rotor system and the new Westland-developed swept-tip composite blades.

WESTLAND LYNX

Main rotor diameter:	42 ft.	
Tail rotor diameter:	7 ft., 3 in.	
Length:	Army:	39 ft., 6 in.
	Navy:	39 ft., 1 in.
Width:	Army:	9 ft., 7.75 in.
	Navy:	12 ft., 3.75 in.
Height:	Army:	12 ft.
	Navy:	11 ft., 9.75 in.
Weight (maximum take-off):	Army:	10,000 lbs.
	Navy:	10,500 lbs.
Cruising speed:	Army:	161 mph
	Navy:	144 mph
Maximum altitude:	Army:	10,600 ft.
	Navy:	8,450 ft.
Range:	Army:	392 miles
	Navy:	368 miles
Date of first flight:	1971	

Left: A Sea Lynx prepares to land aboard a British frigate. The Sea Lynx is the naval version of the Lynx 1. Right: The Royal Navy Sea Lynx proved invaluable to British forces during the Falkland Islands War in 1982, sinking one Argentinean submarine and several surface craft.

WESTLAND LYNX 3

At first glance, the similarity in appearance of the Westland Lynx 3, a derivative of the Lynx family of helicopters, to other Lynx helicopters is undeniable. The major difference in outward appearance is a twin-finned tail design borrowed from the Westland 30 helicopter design. The new tail provides the helicopter with even more precise handling and agility.

The Lynx 3 comes with two Rolls Royce Gem 60 turboshaft engines that can deliver 1,115 horsepower each. This aircraft, which first flew in 1984, sports a new high-technology composite rotor blade design that is up to 40 percent more efficient than conventional rotor blades. These British Experimental Rotor Program tips are made of a wound filament construction; they hold great promise for a variety of future helicopter designs for increased power and performance.

The helicopter's fuselage features a streamlined pod and boom design constructed from a combination of glass fiber composites and light alloy metal. Able to carry 2,204 pounds of fuel, the helicopter has crash resistant/self-sealing fuel bladders built into its fuselage walls. This feature adds greatly to crew survivability should the helicopter be shot down or forced to make an emergency landing.

Although many of the flight dynamics of the basic Lynx have been retained in the Lynx 3, the overall gross weight of the aircraft has increased by more than 27 percent. This dramatic increase is due to more weapons systems firepower. Westland originally designed the Lynx 3 as an antitank helicopter. But Westland is expanding the flight parameters of the aircraft and offering a naval version that can handle both antisubmarine and antiship roles. Depending on the variant, new and advanced avionics enable the helicopter to go tank or ship hunting in virtually all types of weather, day or night. Numerous night vision and target acquisition systems can be mounted in the nose of the chopper,

on the roof above the flight crew, or above the rotor blades.

The armament mainstay for the British Army helicopter is a host of antitank rockets and missiles. The Lynx 3 can carry a full complement of such deadly tank destroyers as the TOW, Hellfire, and HOT missiles. Depending on the helicopter's specific mission, such armaments as folding-fin rockets, cannon pods, machine guns, TV surveillance cameras, chaff dispensers, and air-to-air missiles for self-protection can be added. In the naval version, the latest in computer-controlled torpedoes, homing torpedoes, depth charges, antiship missiles, sonobuoys, dipping sonars, and surface ship radars can be hung on the twin external pylon mounts.

Westland expects the vast array of technological improvements found on the Lynx 3 helicopter to keep the aircraft in production well into the 21st century. The Lynx 3 will be available for export to many nations needing an anti-armor and antisubmarine warfare helicopter of advanced design.

WESTLAND LYNX 3	
Main rotor diameter:	42 ft.
Tail rotor diameter:	8 ft.
Length:	39 ft., 6.8 in.
Width:	10 ft.
Height:	10 ft., 10 in.
Weight (maximum take-off):	13,000 lbs.
Cruising speed:	172 mph
Maximum altitude:	10,600 ft.
Range:	385 miles
Date of first flight:	1984

Left: This Westland Lynx 3 is armed for the antitank role. **Right:** The Lynx 3 is an advanced helicopter that will be able to fulfill various roles from anti-armor to antisubmarine warfare.

In 1978, the British Ministry of Defense selected a Westland Helicopters study that proposed a new aircraft to replace the aging Sea King helicopters serving in the Royal Navy. By keeping the helicopter the same size as the Sea King while incorporating the latest in technological innovations, the overall performance of an antisubmarine warfare (ASW) helicopter would be greatly increased. In 1980, Westland teamed up with the Agusta SpA Helicopter Group of Italy and formed a new company call EH Industries. The new company's purpose was to develop several versions of the new helicopter, all sporting a common design.

The first design from EH Industries is the EH101 helicopter. It will be available in a variety of configurations and tailored for numerous specific military and civilian roles. As flight testing continues, a total of 10 prototype/pre-production aircraft are planned. Conventional in terms of its basic design, the EH101 sports a fuselage made primarily of light alloy metals and a tail and rear section constructed from composites. In the naval version, the aircraft's power comes from three General Electric T700-401A turboshaft engines producing 1,437 horsepower each. In the military and commercial versions, the helicopter will have three General Electric CT7-6 turboshaft engines that deliver 1,649 horsepower each. The five main rotor blades use the British Experimental Rotor Program design and are said to be 40 percent more efficient than conventional blades.

The naval version of the EH101 is designed for both ASW and antiship roles. It will be capable of operating from large or small military ships, oil drilling platforms, shore bases, and from a variety of commercial merchant vessels. For storage when not in use, the helicopter will be compatible with all frigate hangers. The aircraft will feature the latest in technological designs, and it will be able to operate autonomously for up to five hours in all weather. The helicopter will carry the latest in weaponry and detection equipment. While its primary role will be ASW and antiship, the EH101 will also be usable for amphibious operations, search and rescue, supply, fire control, and electronic countermeasures.

The military variant will share the same basic fuselage, rotor, transmission, and flight controls as the naval version. The helicopter will be used for tactical airlift transportation. The rear-loading door and drive-on/drive-off ramp system will enable the aircraft to carry a host of vehicles or cargo. The aircraft will be able to accommodate up to 12,000 pounds of combat gear or 38 combat-ready soldiers. The helicopter can use a sling to carry externally up to 15,000 pounds of gear and supplies.

In the civilian version, the EH101 will feature a crew of two and accommodations for up to 30 passengers, a flight attendant, and baggage storage area. The civilian version will have a range of more than 575 miles and be able to operate in environments ranging from standard commercial airports to oil rigs or downtown city landing zones.

No specific weaponry has been announced for the military transport version of the EH-101, but the naval model will sport armament designed for its ASW and antiship roles. For these missions, look for the EH101 to carry sonars and sonobuoy detection systems, chaff and flare dispenser, and electronic countermeasures gear. Armament will include Penguin Mark 2 Model 7 antiship missiles, Aerospatiale AM39 Exocet antiship missiles, McDonnell Douglas AGM-84 Harpoon antiship missiles, Marte Mark 2 Sea Killer antiship missiles, British Aerospace Sea Eagle cruise missiles or Sea Skua antiship missiles, Mark 46 antisubmarine torpedoes, Sting Ray computer-controlled torpedoes, and machine gun pods.

Production work on the EH101 is divided half and half between Westland and Agusta. Westland is the leader in the civilian version of the helicopter, and Agusta is responsible for the rear-loading military model. The companies are working together to develop the naval version for their respective navies and for export. There will be a final assembly plant in both Italy and Great Britain. Agusta will be responsible for the manufacture of the rear fuselage, rotor head and drive systems, the hydraulic system, and certain parts of the electrical system. Westland is responsible for the cabin, front fuselage, cockpit, and main rotor blade system.

The civilian version of the helicopter is expected to be ready for production as early as 1990 since requirements for a civilian aircraft are easier to fulfill than either the naval or military variant. If aircraft testing and development continue as expected, both the British and Italian Navies should begin accepting the new EH101s around 1993–94.

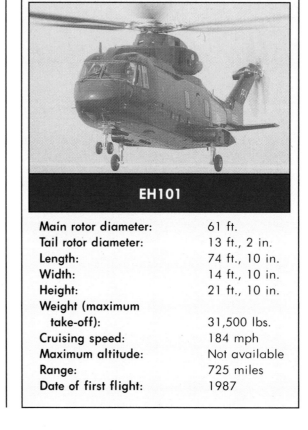

EH101

Main rotor diameter:	61 ft.
Tail rotor diameter:	13 ft., 2 in.
Length:	74 ft., 10 in.
Width:	14 ft., 10 in.
Height:	21 ft., 10 in.
Weight (maximum take-off):	31,500 lbs.
Cruising speed:	184 mph
Maximum altitude:	Not available
Range:	725 miles
Date of first flight:	1987

Left: The EH101 offers the latest in helicopter technology. **Right:** The EH101 was jointly designed by Great Britain and Italy as a multirole military/civilian helicopter.

AEROSPATIALE SA 316B ALOUETTE III

The Alouette series of helicopters from the French company Aerospatiale has roots stretching back to the 1950s. This line of helicopters contributed significantly to the postwar reconstruction of the French aircraft industry. First came the simple, yet proven design of the SE-3120 Alouette Lark. Then came the improved Alouette II Astazou, which boasted a more economical engine and a new centrifugal clutch. Aerospatiale then jumped forward to the Alouette III. Many called it the big sister to the smaller Alouette II, and the resemblance was unmistakable. Although the tail boom had been enclosed and the cabin area expanded to seat seven people, the Alouette III's superb capabilities were definitely and undeniably Aerospatiale. The helicopter became an overnight success.

The Alouette III helicopter first flew in February 1959 and soon proved its flight capabilities through a variety of publicity stunts such as landing and taking off with full maximum loads from atop Mont Blanc in the French Alps. That kind of power spurred sales to a variety of civilian and military marketplaces that operate in hot and/or high-altitude environments, such as Switzerland, Saudi Arabia, India, and Zaire. By the time French production came to an end in May 1985, a total of 1,455 Alouette IIIs had been delivered to civilian and military forces in 74 different countries.

The Alouette III's power, and therefore its success, was derived from a light turbine helicopter powerplant developed by the Turbomeca company—the first engine manufacturer to develop such an engine. This engine, which was used throughout the 316B series of aircraft, developed 870 horsepower and enabled the helicopter to cruise along at a steady 115 miles per hour for ranges in excess of 300 miles.

Even after the French shut down their production lines, numerous other nations continued to produce the Alouette III under license from Aerospatiale. Switzerland built a total of 60 aircraft, and Romania built nearly 200 aircraft in both a civilian and military version. The Romanian military model is called the IAR-317 Airfox. The only group now still producing the Alouette III design is the HAL company of India, which has produced more than 300 helicopters under the Indian designation Chetak.

Since Aerospatiale has ceased production of the aircraft, further improvements to the Alouette III will be limited to modifications by the existing owners. India and Romania have plans for revised avionics, which are rather basic compared with other helicopters in use today. Only a few Alouettes anywhere have much in the way of sophisticated electronics and avionics beyond a basic radio, rudimentary radars, and targeting/sensor systems.

The Alouette III had broad demonstrated capabilities, and it was quickly outfitted with a variety of armaments and weapon systems. In fact, the Alouette II and Alouette III were the first helicopters to be deployed into service carrying guided missiles. Known as the SS-10, this wire-guided antitank missile was carried by the aircraft for several years. Later, the Alouette II and Alouette III were armed with the larger and heavier AS-11. The AS-11 remains the standard armament today, and the Alouette III can carry up to four missiles—two on each side of the aircraft. The weapons operator, who sits beside the pilot, controls firing with the APX-Bezu 260 gyrostabilized sight mounted on the cockpit roof.

Gun weaponry for the Alouette III began with pintle- or tripod-mounted machine guns capable of firing from the side door of the aircraft. A standard item in the weaponry department included the 7.62 millimeter AA-52 gun that had a capacity of 1,000 rounds; it was fired either through the opened or removed door or through a gun portal aperture cut into the door. For heavier firepower, the Alouette III could also be outfitted with a variety of 20mm cannons that had a magazine capacity of up to 480 rounds. Additional weapons systems that can be hung on the outside of the helicopter include a variety of rocket launchers, HOT missiles, Matra Mistral guided missiles, AT-3 Sagger antitank missiles, gun pods, and up to two antisubmarine Mark 44 torpedoes.

Overall, there were few missions in the Alouette III's day that the aircraft couldn't handle. Antitank, antiship, antisubmarine, search and rescue, armed reconnaissance, light attack, or medevac were all part of its job. Today, the Alouette III can continue to fulfill those same roles.

AEROSPATIALE SA 316B ALOUETTE III

Main rotor diameter:	36 ft., 1.75 in.
Tail rotor diameter:	6 ft., 3.25 in.
Length:	32 ft., 11 in.
Width:	8 ft., 6.25 in.
Height:	9 ft., 10 in.
Weight (maximum take-off):	3,630 lbs.
Cruising speed:	115 mph
Maximum altitude:	10,500 ft.
Range:	307 miles
Date of first flight:	1959

Left: The Alouette III is a light utility helicopter built in France and around the world, including India, Romania, Brazil, and Switzerland. **Right:** An Alouette III balances precariously on top of a crag while conducting a search and rescue mission in the French Alps.

AEROSPATIALE SA 341/342 GAZELLE

Development of the agile Aerospatiale Gazelle started in the mid-1960s. The French Army issued a requirement for a light observation helicopter that was faster and even more agile than the helicopters being produced in the Alouette series. There were major differences between the new design, which was designated the X-300, and older helicopter model introductions. A new streamlined fuselage replaced the bubble-type cabin/cockpit area. The open metal latticework tail boom was enclosed and streamlined. A rigid rotor design with glass fiber composite blades, which the German company Messerschmitt-Bolkow-Blohm had pioneered, and an encased—or shrouded—tail rotor blade design called fenestron (fan-in-fin) were added.

Under a 1967 Anglo-French agreement, the Gazelle was co-produced by Aerospatiale and Westland Helicopters. The Gazelle became a mainstay of helicopter technology for both French and British forces. Known as the SA 341, the helicopter soon became a standard for all British services. In the British Army Air Corps, the aircraft was used as an observation ship. In the Royal Air Force and the Navy Fleet Air Arm, the Gazelle was used for helicopter training. The RAF took the attributes of the Gazelle further and used the helicopter as a communications platform and for forward air controller missions.

These early SA 341 Gazelles came with a single Turbomeca Astazou turboshaft engine delivering 590 horsepower, which provided excellent power, performance, and agility for its time. Versions developed and introduced later were improved in their power and are known as the SA 342 model. The SA 342 comes with an engine that develops up to 858 horsepower. Other changes in the newer model include a redesigned fenestron tail rotor, a higher gross take-off weight, and an option for an extended cabin.

The Gazelle's design is conventional. It features an airframe made from light alloy

metals and a glazed cockpit cabin area with transparent moldings held in place by a welded frame. The floor area and center fuselage are made of a honeycomb construction, and the tail boom is a sheet alloy metal design. Blades can be folded if required. Unless ordered otherwise, all Gazelles feature standard skids on which small landing wheels can be added to provide additional taxiing capability. For on-the-water operations and special missions, the helicopter can be fitted with pontoon floats and underwater beacon markers for special forces frogmen.

The basic configuration of the Gazelle consists of a pilot and copilot in side-by-side seating, each with separate systems to fly the aircraft. In the rear, a three-passenger bench can be folded down or removed to accommodate cargo-carrying requirements. In addition to its internal cargo load, the Gazelle

can carry up to 1,500 pounds of additional cargo slung externally from a center fuselage hook. When pressed into search and rescue operations, a hoist able to lift 350 pounds can be installed for lifting downed personnel. When the aircraft is configured for medevac missions, the pilot seat on the left can be removed, creating enough room for two stretchers and a medical attendant.

Gazelles have remained up-to-date in terms of avionics. All are equipped with night-operation packages that include standard radios and additional instrumentation that enables the pilot to fly in virtually all weather conditions. The latest radios, sensors, radars, targeting systems, and communications/enemy detection packages can be retrofitted into the Gazelle for a variety of special mission requirements and options.

When properly outfitted, the Gazelle can perform a variety of attack and fighting mis-

Left: The upward exhaust deflector on this Gazelle indicates that it is the 342M antitank version, which serves with the French ALAT (Army Light Aviation). **Right:** This French ALAT Gazelle, hovering in tree cover, is equipped with four HOT antitank missile launchers.

sions. In its antitank role (known as ALAT, or Army Light Aviation), the helicopter is called the SA 342M and is equipped with a gyro-stabilized sighting system. The system is installed in the roof of the cockpit and is designed with optics that either the pilot or copilot can use when functioning as the gunner. Standard antitank weaponry includes two twin HOT missile launchers, two TOW-2 missile launcher platforms, and the Soviet-made AT-3 Sagger antitank missile. Other standard armament for the helicopter, as determined by its mission, includes a variety of tubular/rail munitions, numerous 20 millimeter cannons, wire-guided missiles, and four different versions of air-to-ground unguided rockets. For self-protection, the Gazelle carries two types of air-defense missiles, the British Blowpipe and the French Matra Mistral. The aircraft is armed with a variety of gun systems, including standard 7.62mm/.50 caliber machine gun options and a 7.62mm minigun that is part of a new turret system that can be jettisoned. The Gazelle can also carry various tactical reconnaissance camera pods.

Nearly 1,200 Gazelles have been produced for 36 nations. The helicopter remains in production and is likely to continue to be upgraded well into the next century.

Left: This helicopter crew loads HOT wire-guided antitank missiles aboard their Gazelle. Right: A highly maneuverable Gazelle antitank helicopter, armed with HOT missiles, emerges from cover.

AEROSPATIALE SA 341/342 GAZELLE

Main rotor diameter:	34 ft., 5.5 in.
Tail rotor diameter:	2 ft., 3.3 in.
Length:	31 ft., .2 in.
Width:	6 ft., 8.5 in.
Height:	10 ft., 5.5 in.
Weight (maximum take-off):	4,410 lbs.
Cruising speed:	161 mph
Maximum altitude:	13,450 ft.
Range:	440 miles
Date of first flight:	1967

148

Left: The antitank version of the Gazelle is equipped with a more powerful 858 horsepower engine. **Right:** The Gazelle was the first to introduce the Aerospatiale-originated fenestron—the shrouded tail rotor. The fenestron design provides more protection for the tail rotor and improves maneuvering capabilities.

AEROSPATIALE SA 365 DAUPHIN/PANTHER

To keep track of all the helicopter variants within the Aerospatiale Dauphin series practically requires a scorecard; there are a host of models and changes within the basic group. The basic aircraft is the SA 365N Dauphin 2, and it is designed as a multirole transport. It remains in full production today.

The helicopter features the distinctive fenestron tail rotor with 11 high-speed blades that are articulated for pitch change. The aircraft also sports a large vertical tail fin and twin horizontal stabilizers as part of the shrouded tail rotor. Power in the basic SA 365 version is derived from two Turbomeca 912 horsepower turboshaft engines, but in the United States Coast Guard version known as the SA 366, power comes from two Avco Lycoming 680 horsepower engines. The four main rotor blades are of a composite design and feature some of the latest technology, including a NOMEX honeycomb filling. The blades attach to a Starflex glass-and-carbon fiber rotor hub that has a quick disconnect pin system for easy replacement and virtually no maintenance.

With the Dauphin's clean aerodynamic fuselage and retractable tricycle landing gear,

Left: The SA 365 Panther is the armed, tactical military version of Aerospatiale's Dauphin. Demonstrating its power and maneuverability, this Panther is in the middle of a barrel roll. Right: The French Navy has purchased a number of Dauphin 2 helicopters for search and rescue missions.

the helicopter offers excellent performance and handling. The helicopter has a standard flight crew of two and, depending on how the aircraft is configured, can carry up to 14 passengers.

For military service, the Dauphin can be used for transport, attack, medevac, and search and rescue. In service with Saudi Arabia, the Dauphin is used in the antiship role and is called the SA 365F/AS.15TT model. Similar in its basic configuration to other Dauphin models, this version is equipped to carry up to 4 AS.15 antiship missiles on lateral pylons. Also in service with the United States Coast Guard, the helicopter is designated the HH-65A Dolphin 2. The Coast Guard has ordered and received 99 of the aircraft for use in short-range recovery duties. The HH-65A can perform search and rescue operations from shore or ship, or drug interdiction missions in conjunction with law enforcement organizations.

The Dauphin 2 is a formidable weapons platform. Depending upon the mission, the Dauphin can be outfitted with a variety of weaponry, including antiship missiles, ship and submarine torpedoes, stabilized day/night gun sights, a 20 millimeter cannon, a 7.62mm machine gun, three types of 68mm rocket pods, quadruple TOW missile launchers, and quadruple HOT missile launchers. The aircraft can also carry submarine sonobuoys, surveillance radars, and camera pods.

Aerospatiale has used the basic design of the Dauphin to introduce a new variant that is built for fighting and surviving in a combat environment. Called the Panther, its basic configuration is nearly identical to the Dauphin, but technical designs have placed a much greater emphasis on battlefield survivability. A production model first flew in 1986, and the Panther went into production in 1988.

To increase strength and reduce weight, the Panther makes much greater use of composite materials than the existing Dauphin heli-

Left: When designing the Panther, a great deal of attention was paid to providing access for ground crews to the aircraft's systems. The engine cover, directly behind the rotor housing shroud, slides back for engine maintenance. Right: The SA 365 Panther can carry a wide variety of weaponry, including the Mistral guided missile, several types of unguided rockets, and 20mm gun pods.

copters. These composites and special radar-absorbing coatings on the helicopter's exterior greatly reduce the aircraft's radar signature, making the Panther difficult to detect. Inside, both crew seats are armored and are designed to withstand crashes or impacts up to 15 G's. Key components around the engines and throughout the many flight control systems are also protected with a variety of armor.

The Panther will serve in a variety of missions that could include assault transport, ground attack, search and rescue, electronic warfare, aerial combat post, medevac, cargo transport, target designation, and armed reconnaissance. Of course, the Panther can car-ry the entire assortment of weaponry available on the basic Dauphin helicopter as well as additional sensors and electronics.

At present, nearly 400 Dauphins have been built or ordered. This number also includes aircraft that are in production in China, where the helicopter is called the Harbin Z-9. A total of 37 different nations, including Chile, France, and Ireland, use Dauphin variants in many civilian and military applications. Competition in the multipurpose helicopter arena is fierce, but the Dauphin and Panther have established solid reputations for performance and versatility. Production is expected to continue well into the late 1990s and beyond.

AEROSPATIALE SA 365 DAUPHIN/PANTHER

Main rotor diameter:	39 ft., 2 in.
Tail rotor diameter:	3 ft., 7.5 in.
Length:	38 ft., 2 in.
Width:	10 ft., 6.5 in.
Height:	11 ft., 6.5 in.
Weight (maximum take-off):	9,039·lbs.
Cruising speed:	176 mph
Maximum altitude:	11,810 ft.
Range:	530 miles
Date of first flight:	1972

Left: This SA 365 Panther, with its retractable landing gear down, makes a landing approach. **Right:** The Panther is an extremely maneuverable and fast helicopter with a top speed of 184 mph.

Left: The Dauphin/Panther's "Starflex" rotor system is clearly visible. A complex combination of carbon, glass fiber, and half steel balls and sockets eliminates hinges and the need for lubrication. **Right:** The French Dauphin/Panther is rapidly gaining adherents worldwide. The U.S. Coast Guard recently purchased the Dauphin 2 and designated it the HH-65.

AEROSPATIALE AS 350/355 ECUREUIL

The AS 350/355 Ecureuil, or Squirrel, was originally designed as a successor to the Aerospatiale Alouette series. The AS 350/355 Ecureuil is similar in size to the SA 341/342 Gazelle but features a completely new design sporting technological improvements that are designed to decrease operating costs, maintenance requirements, and noise.

The AS 350, a light utility multirole helicopter, flew for the first time in June 1974 with one 641 horsepower Turbomeca turboshaft engine. The AS 355 is a twin-engine version of the same aircraft that is marketed in the United States as the Twinstar helicopter and elsewhere throughout the world as the Ecureuil 2. Power for the AS 355 comes from two Allison 250-C20F turboshaft engines that develop 420 horsepower each. The engines give the Ecureuil the power to climb at a rate of nearly 1,300 feet per minute. Recently, Aerospatiale upgraded the powerplant package and is now producing the Ecureuil series with new 509 horsepower Turbomeca TM 319 engines.

Left: The single-engine AS 350 Ecureuil was designed and built as a successor to the Gazelle. This Ecureuil is equipped with Mistral missiles for the antitank role. **Right:** The twin-engine AS 355 Ecureuil is known as the Twinstar in the United States but as the Ecureuil 2 in the rest of the world.

Both the 350 and 355 versions feature a rotor hub made of a glass-and-carbon fiber composite design called Starflex. The simple gearbox features only nine gearwheels, and the simple transmission has nine bearings. These previous features, coupled with three advanced design rotor blades that are manufactured by a computer-controlled production process, make the aircraft economical to operate and easy to maintain. The fuselage is covered with a thermoformed plastic instead of light alloy honeycomb panels. The aircraft is configured for a crew of two.

For civilian use, the aircraft is ideal for oil platform transportation, executive transport, news reporting, and law enforcement patrols. The Ecureuil can accommodate four passengers. For cargo transport, the helicopter can be ordered with a large sliding door on each side, removable seats, and an exterior cargo hoist hook. For rescue operations, an electric rescue hoist is also available. A water drop fire fighting system and an agricultural spray tank system are also offered.

In the military arena, both the AS 350 and AS 355 feature advanced electronics that can be tailored to order. In addition to standard flight equipment packages, the Ecureuil can be equipped with full infrared instrumentation, radar altimeter, night-vision goggles, and electronic targeting sensors. The aircraft can be used for armed reconnaissance, light attack, target designation, search and rescue, and cargo transport.

Virtually all military versions of the helicopter are equipped with pylon adapters and attachments that allow weaponry to be pointed only straight ahead. This small lightweight helicopter can be armed to the

Left: This television news team flies an AS 350 Ecureuil. **Right:** The Ecureuil is fast, light, and extremely maneuverable, which makes it well-suited for the anti-tank role.

teeth for a variety of light attack missions. In the anti-armor role, the aircraft can carry twin HOT or TOW wire-guided missile launchers on each side. For soft targets, rocket launchers, machine guns, and cannon pods are attached. Helicopters will have to be able to fight and survive aerial combat, and the Ecureuil can be outfitted with such air-to-air defensive missiles as the Matra Mistral and General Dynamics Stinger.

The AS 350/355, a high-speed and excellent flier, is a popular choice for more than 30 nations, including Singapore, Australia, and Denmark; some 2,000 AS 350/355 helicopters have been ordered for both civilian and military use. The Ecureuil is an ideal choice for a variety of light and tactical military applications. With the twin TM-319 engines now available on the AS 355, orders are expected to remain steady for many years to come. Production lines will continue to operate both in France and under license in Brazil. In Brazil, the AS 350, built by Helibras, is called the CH-50 Esquilo, and two versions of the twin engine AS 355 are designated the CH-55 or VH-55 Esquilo.

AEROSPATIALE AS 350/355 ECUREUIL		
Main rotor diameter:	35 ft., .75 in.	
Tail rotor diameter:	6 ft., 1.25 in.	
Length:	35 ft., 10.5 in.	
Width:	5 ft., 10.75 in.	
Height:	10 ft., 11.5 in.	
Weight (maximum take-off):	AS 350: 4,850 lbs.	
	AS 355: 5,732 lbs.	
Cruising speed:	AS 350: 144 mph	
	AS 355: 139 mph	
Maximum altitude:	15,000 ft.	
Range:	AS 350: 407 miles	
	AS 355: 437 miles	
Date of first flight:	1974	

Left: This close-up shows the Mistral fire-and-forget rocket launchers mounted on the pylons of an AS 350 Ecureuil. Right: This Ecureuil mounts a gyrostabilized day/night sight above the cockpit.

Left: Like other French antitank helicopters, the Ecureuil antitank version has an upward deflector mounted on the engine exhaust. **Right:** The Ecureuil 2 helicopter is considered by many to be the ideal helicopter for light transport, passenger service, or other services, such as checking on lighthouses.

AEROSPATIALE AS 332 SUPER PUMA

The Puma, Super Puma, and Super Puma Mark II series of helicopters from Aerospatiale result from taking a good design and making continual modifications and refinements. The improvements have kept the aircraft current for a variety of missions. Today's AS 332 Super Puma, its origins dating back to the mid-1960s, may superficially look like the earlier SA 330 Puma, but there are many significant improvements and differences.

Although the older Puma was a fine helicopter in many respects, Aerospatiale decided in 1974 that an improved aircraft would be more competitive in the military and civilian marketplaces. The Super Puma, first flown in September 1978, was the result; production models were flying by February 1980. The Puma was originally designed as an all-weather tactical medium-lift helicopter for the French Army ALAT (Army Light Aviation). Many small changes that improved crash safety, reduced operational noise, decreased maintenance requirements, and increased payload capacity helped turn the

Left: The Aerospatiale AS 332 Super Puma is powered by two 1,780 horsepower turboshaft engines. Right: The AS 332 Super Puma serves in a variety of roles with navies around the world, including search and rescue and antisubmarine warfare.

Puma into the Super Puma. Important power increases in the engines offered significant performance improvements over the original Puma. The Super Puma carries two internally mounted Turbomeca Makila IA1 engines, raising power to 1,877 horsepower from 1,780 horsepower.

Five modern versions of the Super Puma are available today. The AS 332B is the basic military version. It is capable of carrying up to 21 combat troops with its crew of two. The AS 332F is the naval version and features a deck-landing assistance device for ship-borne operations, special anticorrosion metal treatments, and a folding tail rotor pylon for compact storage. The naval version is built for everything from antiship and antisubmarine warfare to search and rescue. The AS 332L is a civilian version of the Super Puma. The cabin, which can accommodate up to 24 passengers, has been stretched 2.5 feet and features two additional windows as well as increased fuel capacity. The AS 332M features the extended cabin of the AS 332L but is built as a military transport aircraft that can haul up to 25 combat soldiers.

The fifth version is the new Super Puma Mark II. The Mark II features an improved new main rotor system that will enhance performance and economy without changing or modifying the aircraft's basic powerplants. Several significant modifications have resulted in a new and lighter design that complements the increase of 1.6 feet in fuselage length. The longer fuselage is necessary to accommodate the slightly longer rotor blades. In addition to increased performance, the Mark II will offer increased range, an autopilot feature with new cockpit displays, and additional avionics. The Super Puma Mark II is expected to begin production in 1990.

A future change may include the battlefield surveillance system Orchidee (Obersavtoire Radar Coherent Heliporte d'Investigation Des Elements Ennemis). This system will be used to coordinate French ground

Left: This AS 332 Super Puma wears the colors of the Singapore Air Force. **Right:** The AS 332 Super Puma serves with French military crews throughout the world.

forces. Orchidee uses a highly advanced doppler radar system to locate enemy troop concentrations, convoys, or movements as far as 60 miles behind enemy lines while the helicopter itself is more than 25 miles inside its own lines and operating at an altitude of almost 10,000 feet. The surveillance radar device is mounted under the rear of the helicopter's cabin area and swings down into place via a rotating mount. This system has been in operational field testing since 1986 and could begin appearing by the mid-1990s on new helicopters ordered by the French Army. It is anticipated the French will replace their aging fleet of SA 330 Puma helicopters with Orchidee-equipped Super Pumas.

While most Super Pumas are unarmed, they are heavily laden with a host of avionics and defensive devices. Featuring the latest in communications gear, radars, sensors, and even sonars, the Super Puma can fill a vari-

ety of military missions. If an armed version is desired, the Super Puma can be equipped to carry such modern weaponry as a 20 millimeter cannon, machine guns, rocket launchers, Mistral missiles, reconnaissance camera pods, doppler radar systems for battlefield surveillance, two Sea Skua or Exocet antiship missiles, and up to two parachute-equipped acoustic antiship torpedoes. When used for antisubmarine warfare operations, the Super Puma can carry sonobuoys, dipped sonar detectors, and the latest in antisubmarine torpedo weaponry.

More than 350 AS 332 Super Pumas have been delivered to or are on order by nearly 40 military forces from around the world, including Singapore, Argentina, and Oman. Production is taking place under license in Indonesia, and assembly is taking place under license in Spain. The Super Puma series of helicopters will continue to be one of the

most widely used medium-lift models for many years to come. Aerospatiale officials believe there are several future modifications and variants that will keep the aircraft current well into the 21st century.

AEROSPATIALE AS 332 SUPER PUMA	
Main rotor diameter:	51 ft., 2.25 in.
Tail rotor diameter:	10 ft.
Length:	50 ft., 11.5 in.
Width:	12 ft., 5.25 in.
Height:	16 ft., 1.75 in.
Weight (maximum take-off):	19,841 lbs.
Cruising speed:	156 mph
Maximum altitude:	11,480 ft.
Range:	384 miles
Date of first flight:	1978

Left: The Super Puma's complex cockpit of controls and instrumentation systems is amply seen here. The pilot sits in the left-hand seat. **Right:** Most Super Pumas are unarmed, since the craft's primary military function is in the transportation or utility role.

172

Left: The Super Puma can be configured to carry a wide variety of weapons to support ground forces or to serve in the antisubmarine and antiship role. **Right:** More than 370 Super Pumas have been built and sold worldwide.

MESSERSCHMITT-BOLKOW-BLOHM BO 105

The concept of the Messerschmitt-Bolkow-Blohm (MBB) Bo 105 helicopter was launched in 1962. It was one of the first major postwar aircraft design and development programs by the Federal Republic of Germany (West Germany). The government contract called for an advanced rotor design that would feature a rigid hub and composite blades. The idea behind the rigid, or hingeless, hub concept was to keep the blades from flapping and dragging. The blades were to be cantilevered from the hub itself

and would be capable of changes in pitch only. The advantages of such a system ranged from increased aircraft stability to greater maneuverability. The reduction in rotor blade/hub moving parts would also improve maintenance.

While research into the rigid hub design continued, various Bo 105 prototypes were flown that used existing technology. In February 1967, the first helicopter using advanced design features flew. Its technology included a rigid titanium hub with feathering hinges

only and flexible glass fiber blades. Since 1970, all Bo 105s have featured NACA 23012 "droop snoot" rotor blades.

Except for the hub and rotor blade, the helicopter is conventional in design. The fuselage and tail boom are of a light alloy. The fuselage features a titanium deck under the helicopter's engines and glass-fiber-reinforced cowling panels. The landing gear consists of simple skids to which emergency quick-inflation flotation bags can be attached for on-the-water operations.

Left: The Bo 105 light helicopter was the first helicopter designed and built in Germany in the postwar period. **Right:** The Bo 105 was designed to be a light utility helicopter with military applications.

In the standard configuration, the pilot and copilot sit side by side. Virtually the entire fuselage behind the seats is available for cargo and baggage, and the aircraft has large clamshell doors in the rear and two large sliding doors on the side for easy access to the cargo area. The rear bench seat can be removed to carry cargo or stretchers. In armed versions, the rear cargo area is usually filled with mission equipment. All versions have excellent external lighting systems for night landings and operations. Various optional equipment packages for tailoring the aircraft to a variety of missions include external loudspeaker, rescue hoist, cargo loading hook, auxiliary fuel tanks in the cargo compartment, fuel jettison system, and folding main rotor.

The Bo 105 features two Allison 250-C20B turbine engines delivering 420 horsepower each, which gives the aircraft a very high rate of climb and excellent maneuverability. The Bo 105 can climb at 600 feet per minute at takeoff and maintain a steady rate of climb at maximum power of a very quick 1,575 feet per minute.

The aircraft is able to accept a variety of armament. Main armament for the antitank attack version includes up to six HOT missiles or eight TOW missiles. For missions involving "soft targets," such as troop concentrations, armored personnel carriers, military convoys, and covert/special forces operations, most weapons stores can be hung on external hangers. Options include nearly the entire spectrum of air-to-ground rockets, 20 millimeter cannons, various machine guns and machine gun pods, Stingers, and chaff and flare dispensers.

In the communications and avionics department, the Bo 105 can be fitted with virtually all state-of-the-art equipment. Complete day-and-night, all-weather avionics enable the pilot to operate the aircraft under almost any adverse conditions of darkness and weather. For combat, the aircraft is equipped

Left: This Bo 105 is equipped with six HOT guided antitank missiles. Right: For protection against erosion from airborne particles, the Bo 105 has a forged titanium rotor hub and strips of titanium on the leading edge of all rotor blades.

with a variety of sensors, optics, and self-protection devices, which can include thermal imaging equipment, night goggles for the pilot and copilot, laser range finders, stabilized gun sights, and electronic countermeasure systems.

Designed as a multirole light helicopter, the Bo 105's various missions have included antitank, observation, armed reconnaissance, search and rescue, and law enforcement. The Bo 105 continues in production today, and more than 1,200 have been built and delivered to 37 different nations, including Mexico, Sweden, Spain, and Canada. For the future, MBB plans to offer upgrades to the existing fleet of helicopters. Upgrades will include engines with more power, new rotor blades for increased performance, and other changes that will increase the aircraft's take-off weight. The additional payload capacity could be used to carry more fuel, additional armaments, or high-load weights. Upgrades will begin in 1990, and all indications are that this small and agile helicopter will continue in military and civilian service for many years to come.

MESSERSCHMITT-BOLKOW-BLOHM BO 105	
Main rotor diameter:	32 ft., 3.5 in.
Tail rotor diameter:	6 ft., 2.75 in.
Length:	28 ft., 1 in.
Width:	8 ft., 3.5 in.
Height:	9 ft., 10 in.
Weight (maximum take-off):	5,291 lbs.
Cruising speed:	150 mph
Maximum altitude:	17,000 ft.
Range:	357 miles
Date of first flight:	1967

Left: The twin 420 horsepower Allison turboshaft engines provide a maximum sustained cruising speed of 150 mph. **Right:** These West German Army Bo 105 helicopters equipped with Mistral missiles provide a potent antitank helicopter force.

MESSERSCHMITT-BOLKOW-BLOHM/KAWASAKI BK 117

The Messerschmitt-Bolkow-Blohm/Kawasaki BK 117 combines German and Japanese aeronautic talents and abilities. In 1974, Kawasaki of Japan was working on a seven- to nine-passenger helicopter designated the KH-7; at the same time, the West German firm of Messerschmitt-Bolkow-Blohm (MBB) was working on a similar design called the BK 107. Realizing they would be competing head-to-head, the two companies agreed in 1977 to jointly produce a helicopter called the BK 117. It was agreed MBB would produce the main and tail rotors, control systems, tail boom, landing skids, engine compartment firewalls and cowlings, and hydraulics as well as oversee the integration of all these systems. Kawasaki would make the fuselage, transmission, electrical and fuel systems, and all other standard items required for flight.

Only a limited number of the helicopters have been manufactured to date, and the actual process of building the aircraft is the single-source method. Each company produces the components it has developed, and those parts are then exchanged for production parts made by the partner. Two final assembly lines are currently in use: MBB uses its plant in Donauworth and Kawasaki uses its Gifu factory.

The BK 117 can seat seven, and in many respects, the BK 117 is an enlarged Bo 105 helicopter. It uses the Kawasaki transmission system, but the main rotor group is almost identical to the latest Bo 105 offering. The aircraft features larger blades that are fitted with anti-vibration weights. The antierosion strips on the blades are of stainless steel.

The BK 117 features a nose section that is long, wide, and very streamlined. The tail boom is thin and streamlined and features a horizontal stabilizer with delta-shaped fins that are sharply inclined for greater stability. Except for the horizontal stabilizer, which is made from composites, the aircraft's airframe and primary structure are made of conven-

tional metal alloys. Several areas of the helicopter's skin are reinforced with Kevlar for strength.

Two Avco Lycoming LTS 101-650B-1 turboshaft engines that deliver 550 horsepower each power this multipurpose helicopter. The aircraft can climb at nearly 2,350 feet per minute. The BK 117 has two independent fuel-feeding systems and a common main fuel tank that holds 160 gallons.

Avionics and state-of-the-art communications equipment are available, as well as all such modern navigation aids as laser/doppler system, radar altimeter, transponder, Navstar, Loran, and AHRS (Attitude/Heading Reference System). The military version, called the BK 117A-3M, will have weapons control avionics, a host of targeting computers, electronic warfare equipment and jam-

mers, and either a roof-mounted stabilized sight or mast-mounted sight system.

The BK 117 can carry a variety of armament options, including either HOT or TOW missile antitank weaponry in a quad launcher configuration. The aircraft can be fitted with 2.75-inch folding fin rockets, 68 millimeter rockets, CASA 80mm rockets, two Stinger air-to-air missile launchers, and the SURA 81mm rocket system. Gun systems range from standard Rheinmetall or Oerlikon 20mm cannons to General Electric 7.62mm miniguns.

In the military configuration, the BK 117 would sport dual pilot controls. If stripped of all military weapons systems, the helicopter could carry up to 11 combat soldiers.

Overall, the BK 117 shows much promise as either an armed or unarmed multipurpose helicopter. The aircraft can function in a variety of roles, including fire fighting, law enforcement, cargo transport, and search and rescue. However, interest has been somewhat limited; fewer than 50 commercial models and no military versions have been built or ordered to date. But the BK 117 continues to be used as a test-bed for a variety of upgraded systems, including a recently exhibited all-composite airframe version.

MESSERSCHMITT-BOLKOW-BLOHM/KAWASAKI BK 117	
Main rotor diameter:	36 ft., 1 in.
Tail rotor diameter:	6 ft., 5 in.
Length:	32 ft., 6.25 in.
Width:	5 ft., 3 in.
Height:	11 ft., .25 in.
Weight (maximum take-off):	7,055 lbs.
Cruising speed:	158 mph
Maximum altitude:	15,000 ft.
Range:	363 miles
Date of first flight:	1979

Left: This BK 117 is armed with two 19-round launchers for 2.75 inch free-flight rockets. **Right:** The Lucas Aerospace .50 caliber machine gun in its chin-mount is clearly visible under the BK 117's nose.

AGUSTA A 109A MARK II

Agusta of Italy has been manufacturing helicopters since 1952, when the company was first licensed to produce the Bell 47. Since then, Agusta has produced a variety of helicopters using designs from Bell, Boeing, and Sikorsky. The A 109 series, however, is Agusta's own design and has established itself as one of the premiere helicopters in the light multirole class. The A 109 first flew in 1971 and is now manufactured in a variety of models, including civilian, general military, forward observation, and a "high and hot" (high operating altitude and hot climate temperature) export version.

Conventional in its overall design, the A 109 is a high-speed, high-performance helicopter that can fulfill a variety of light helicopter missions. Except for the "high and hot" A 109K version, all A 109 aircraft share the same basic engines, two Allison 250-C20B turboshafts that produce 400 horsepower. The helicopter features a fully articulated four-bladed single main rotor. Retractable tricycle landing gear creates an aerodynamically "clean" aircraft that enables it to cruise at speeds of up to 178 miles per hour. The basic A 109A Mark II is made of light metal alloys and is constructed in four main sections that are joined together.

In its standard configuration, the A 109 carries a crew of two and up to six passengers. In the VIP mode, the layout reduces seating to four or five and adds such amenities as wet bar and sound system. Currently, civilian versions are used for water dropping for fire fighters, executive VIP transportation, medical life-flights, news reporting, law enforcement, and cargo hauling. Depending on the aircraft's mission, additional equipment can include external cargo sling, a rescue hoist, water bomber container, stretcher carriers, and a host of specialized interior packages.

The military version of the aircraft features many of the same attributes as the civilian version. Most military versions also include complete dual instrumentation and controls, sliding doors, armored seats for the crew, main rotor and tail rotor brake, high-load cargo floor, and external supports for outside cargo lift.

Depending upon the mission, the military version of the A 109A Mark II helicopter can be configured several ways. The "Aerial Scout" version can be armed with a variety of weaponry and pressed into service as a fast and agile reconnaissance aircraft. The "Light Attack Armor" version is designed to go after tanks, armored columns, and other hard targets with antitank weaponry that includes the TOW and Mathogo missiles. In the "Light Attack" role, the aircraft carries a combination of machine guns, remote gun pods, and various rocket launchers. The "Command and Control" model can also be armed with rockets and machine guns but is usually lightly armed. This model is used for target designation and directing other helicopters in the battlefield attack. The "Utility/Emergency Medical Service" helicopter can be configured to carry up to seven combat soldiers or up to two stretcher patients with medical assistance personnel. This version can also support a rescue hoist and a cargo hook for external loads. The "Mirach" version carries two Mirach 100 Remote Piloted Vehicles that can be used for battlefield surveillance, reconnaissance, targeting, electronic countermeasures, direct attack targeting, and decoying enemy fire. The "ECM" model is the electronic countermeasures and electronic warfare version. It hosts the latest in sophisticated avionics and electronic systems, chaff dispensers in the tail section, and weapons dictated by mission needs.

In the naval model, the helicopter will usually feature a nonretractable landing gear, additional radars, automatic navigation system, tie-down/anchorage points for deck securing, and additional fuel tank capacity. The naval model is used for antiship missions, electronic warfare, standoff missile guidance, antisubmarine warfare patrol, over-the-horizon reconnaissance, and search and rescue operations. In this version, the helicopter can be armed with antiship missiles, antisubmarine torpedoes, sonobuoys, and air-to-air antiaircraft missiles.

Two additional versions of the A 109 are also offered and remain in production. The A 109 EOA is being procured by the Italian Army as a new advanced observation helicopter. The lengthened nose can accommodate additional avionics and sensor packages. The EOA version also has up-rated engines, crash-survival fuel tanks, and a variety of armament options.

The Agusta A 109K, developed as the "high and hot" variant, was built for the Middle East and Africa. Some major differences include up-rated Turbomeca Arriel IK turboshaft engines, an up-rated transmission, composite blades with a hardened surface that resists chipping and damage caused by sand, and a variety of selected weaponry.

Overall, the A 109 series continues to be one of Agusta's most successful designs. With the wide variety of models offered and sales that have already topped 300, the A 109 will be around for a long time.

AGUSTA A 109A MARK II

Main rotor diameter:	36 ft., 1 in.
Tail rotor diameter:	6 ft., 8 in.
Length:	35 ft., 1.5 in.
Width:	4 ft., 8 in.
Height:	10 ft., 10 in.
Weight (maximum take-off):	5,732 lbs.
Cruising speed:	178 mph
Maximum altitude:	18,000 ft.
Range:	368 miles
Date of first flight:	1971

The Agusta A109 was designed and built to be a multirole light helicopter capable of performing a variety of military missions.

AGUSTA-BELL 212

Since Agusta has been a Bell Helicopter licensee since the early 1950s, the Agusta-Bell 212 (AB 212) twin engine utility transport helicopter was a natural for production by the Italian firm. The helicopter has remained in production since the first one flew in 1971. The AB 212 has electronics and avionics modified to meet the needs of the Italian Army as well as other European military and civilian customers.

The AB 212 is conventional in design. It sports two 1,290 horsepower Pratt & Whitney Canada PT6T-3B Twin Turbo Pac turboshaft engines coupled to a combining gearbox with a single output shaft. Should one engine fail, the remaining engine can deliver up to 800 horsepower of power to maintain flight. The aircraft has a maximum rate of climb of 1,860 feet per minute.

The basic AB 212, when used for land operation missions, can be armed with a variety of ground and air attack weaponry. For protection against the air attack, the standard package would be quadruple Bofors RBS-70 antiaircraft missile launchers. For ground attack, the helicopter would carry a variety of rocket launchers, machine guns and machine gun pods, 20 millimeter cannons, parachuted mines, and surveillance cameras.

Agusta has much experience manufacturing helicopters designed for operation from small sea-decks for antisubmarine warfare (ASW) operations. The AB 212 was a natural base model in which to incorporate a great deal of current ASW technology, and a variant of the basic AB 212 is the AB 212 ASW.

Aside from some structural strengthening to allow for deck tie-downs on ships, the airframe of the AB 212 ASW is similar to the civilian and military versions. Since its primary mission is to search out and destroy enemy submarines, much of the avionics, equipment, sensors, and weaponry is tailored for this role. Inside, the pilot and copilot/weapons operator have dual control systems for the aircraft and the weapons systems. Designed for all weather and day/night operations, the ASW model has the latest in communications and navigation equipment.

Using a dunking sonar system from Bendix, the AB 212 ASW can listen for submarines to depths down to 1,000 feet. With automatic flight controls, the aircraft can remain steady regardless of wind or sea conditions. Once a submarine has been located, the aircraft can process targeting information and launch one of its two antisubmarine Motofides 244AS torpedoes or depth charges.

When operating against surface ships, the naval helicopter uses a Ferranti Seaspray surveillance radar located above the cockpit. This radar can reach to long-range distances in search of ships. Weaponry against surface targets might include Sea Skua or Marte Mark 2 antiship missiles. When operating as a standoff missile-guidance platform, a specially equipped AB 212 version can provide passive guidance for the long-range ship-launched Otomat II surface-to-surface missile. For protection against detection and targeting, the helicopter has a host of electronic countermeasures.

According to Agusta, the AB 212 and the AB 212 ASW are expected to remain in production for years to come. Various electronic and avionic upgrades will increase the helicopter's overall fighting capabilities.

AGUSTA-BELL 212	
Main rotor diameter:	48 ft.
Tail rotor diameter:	8 ft., 6 in.
Length:	42 ft., 4.75 in.
Width:	9 ft., 4.5 in.
Height:	12 ft., 10 in.
Weight (maximum take-off):	11,200 lbs.
Cruising speed:	127 mph
Maximum altitude:	17,000 ft.
Range:	307 miles
Date of first flight:	1971

Left: Although these AB 212s may look like Bell Hueys, they are actually built by Agusta under license from Bell. Right: The Italian-built AB 212 serves in a variety of roles with the Italian military and with civilian customers around the globe.

AGUSTA 129 MONGOOSE

In 1972, the Italian Army published requirements for a light helicopter to perform in an antitank role. The Agusta 129 Mongoose met or exceeded the required characteristics. The Agusta 129 is the only European attack helicopter flying to date. The aircraft is a multirole helicopter that carries an amazing range of weaponry and is capable of flying in any weather or at night.

The Agusta 129 is a twin-engine, four-bladed attack helicopter, built largely of composite materials. Two Rolls Royce GEM 2 Mark 1004 engines, each producing 895 horsepower, power the helicopter. Vents in the engine exhausts mix cold air with the hot exhaust for infrared suppression. The engines are controlled by digital electronic controls, are simple in design, and can be changed under field conditions in 30 minutes. The engines drive the transmission directly at 27,500 revolutions per minute, eliminating the need for a reduction gear and increasing the helicopter's survivability. The transmission can operate for 30 minutes after loss of lubrication.

The main rotor (Agusta-designed and patented) is four-bladed; each blade is mounted on a single elastomeric (synthetic rubber or plastic) bearing. The blades themselves are made of NOMEX with leading edge strips of steel-titanium, and the blade tips are designed to produce a low-noise profile. The main rotor blades can withstand hits from .50 caliber or 23 millimeter weapons and can cut branches up to five inches thick. The NOMEX blades can also withstand the severe abrasion from trees, power lines, and other material occasioned when flying close to the ground.

Tandem seating for the pilot and weapons operator provides excellent visibility in all directions. The pilot sits behind and above the weapons operator, and both are surrounded by armored panels and protected by Martin-Baker armored seats. The helicopter has been designed for crash survivability based on

United States Department of Defense military standards. In the event of a violent impact, the cabin will not be crushed by more than 20 percent of its volume, and the Martin-Baker seats will reduce an impact of 43-G force to an impact of 15 G's or less. The airframe contains roll bars, and the main rotor is well supported. The fuel tanks are self-sealing, and the fixed tricycle landing gear can survive an impact of 32.8 feet per second.

To protect against ballistic damage, all flight control linkages are protected within the rotary mast, which also ensures against icing and reduces radar reflectivity. Provision has been made for a mast-mounted sight that can be used for aiming rockets, machine guns, or lasers while on attack or scout missions.

The Mongoose has two separate fuel systems with cross-feeds to each self-sealing tank, three hydraulic servocontrol systems (one a backup for the tail rotor), and a backup fly-by-wire for the main and tail rotors. Should everything fail at the same time, the pilot can still control the aircraft through a mechanical foot pedal system.

The Harris Corporation's Government Information Systems Division of Melbourne, Florida, has developed a fully Integrated Multiplex System based on two redundant interfaced computers. The computers manage the helicopter's electronics and flight controls by dividing them into seven basic subsystems and then displaying to the pilot and weapons operator only the data needed. This data includes communication, navigation, autopilot, fly-by-wire, engine performance, transmission and hydraulic systems conditions, fuel, electrical, aircraft performance, cautions and warnings, sight and Pilot Night Vision, and fire control, not including TOW missiles.

The pilot and weapons operator are as well equipped for combat as state-of-the-art technology can provide. The Mongoose uses Honeywell's Night Vision System, which uses Forward Looking Infra Red with a display for

both pilot and weapons operator. Both pilot and weapons operator wear the Honeywell Integrated Helmet Display and Sight System, which is similar to that used in the AH-64 Apache. The Mongoose can be configured for a number of other roles (scouting, naval tasks, or tactical transport) as well as air-to-air combat when fitted with either the Mistral or the Stinger missile systems.

AGUSTA 129 MONGOOSE

Main rotor diameter:	39 ft., .6 in.
Tail rotor diameter:	7 ft., 4.25 in.
Length:	40 ft., 3 in.
Width:	11 ft., 9.6 in.
Height:	10 ft., 10.5 in.
Weight (maximum take-off):	9,039 lbs.
Cruising speed:	161 mph
Maximum altitude:	7,840 ft.
Range:	390 miles
Date of first flight:	1983

Left: This Agusta A129 Mongoose returns from a mission with empty free-flight rocket and Hellfire missile launchers. **Right:** The Agusta A129, designed and built in Italy, is the first European-designed-and-built antitank helicopter.